The Life

of a

Navy Wife

By

Jasa L. Bowser-Shaw

PublishAmerica
Baltimore

First printing

ISBN: 1-4137-6085-6
PUBLISHED BY PUBLISHAMERICA, LLLP
www.publishamerica.com
Baltimore

Printed in the United States of America

Dedication

This book is dedicated to all those who have believed in me as a writer, a mother, a daughter, a sister, a wife, and a friend. 143

To my loving husband, Chip:

Thank you for never questioning my endeavors, for letting me be myself, and for always being a supportive husband. I also thank you for giving me two beautiful children and a life full of adventures. I am proud to say I am your wife.

To my mother, Jeanne:

who has always believed I could do great things and pushed me to pursue my love of writing. I would not be writing this today without your positive energy.

To my father, Lenne:

for always teaching me to dream big and reach for the stars. Your encouragement has guided me along the way and continues to today and every day of my life.

I also thank the Lord for giving me two charismatic children, Cody and McKenna.

Cody: Thank you for being the best son a mom could ask for. Every day you amaze me with your maturity and love. I know you will do great things with your life.

McKenna: So sweet and so feisty at the same time. I love you for that and can't wait to see how you grow up to be an independent young woman.

To my big brothers, both on earth and in heaven:

I love you and thank you for the memories you have given me as protective, loving brothers. You are in my thoughts every day from morning 'til night.

Table of Contents

Prologue: Married Young, My Navy
                    Journey Begins — 7
Chapter 1   Married and Graduating High School — 11
Chapter 2   Submarine Wife — 16
Chapter 3   Communication with Home — 21
Chapter 4   First Deployment and First Wes Pac — 27
Chapter 5   Submarine Life — 32
Chapter 6   The Benefit of Separating Work
                    and Personal Life — 36
Chapter 7   Be a Proud Navy Wife — 44
Chapter 8   If It's Going to Happen, It's Going to
                    Happen When He's Deployed — 48
Chapter 9   Care Packages — 60
Chapter 10   Commissary Patience — 69
Chapter 11   The Aviation Community — 78
Chapter 12   Navy Wife Humor — 83
Chapter 13   Don't Be in a Hurry Going on Base — 87
Chapter 14   Do You Know the Flag Rules
                    and Regulations? — 90
Chapter 15   Then and Now — 106

Prologue

Married Young, My Navy Journey Begins

My journey as a Navy wife takes me back to the tender age of 12 when I met my future husband. I won't go into too much detail, but I get asked a lot how Chip and I met because we married so young. So, let me share some hopefully interesting tidbits with you.

My family owned a Native American gift shoppe in Pennsylvania, in the outskirts of Pittsburgh. Every summer we would go to the "country" and set up at a rodeo about 2 hours away. One summer, during the beginning of the rodeo, two cute boys came up to my parents' jewelry stand and were standing by my Aunt Renee who was there to help out. She asked how she could help the boys.

The boys said they were "just looking."

My aunt, being a spunky soul, said, "Are you looking at the jewelry or my niece?"

They grinned and muttered, "Your niece," quietly. Both dropped their heads sheepishly.

She asked them how old they were; they said, "15," in unison.

My aunt let them know they were too old for her niece (me) who was only 12, and they should be on their way. They walked off, and in the distance Lee Greenwood's song "Proud To Be An American" began to play to signal the beginning of the rodeo. The boys were gone, and I was embarrassed but giggly and giddy when I was telling her that I thought the redhead was kind of cute. At intermission, the two boys returned.

The redhead came over to the stand yet again (a glutton for punishment!), and he said to my aunt, "Uhm, I am really only 12." She said with a sparkle in her eye, "Well, son, now you are not only a liar, but you are STILL too old for my niece. Be on your way." The next 10 minutes the boys stood off in the distance, and I stood by my aunt. Neither knowing how we could find a way to talk...we just smiled at each other. After the rodeo, the cute redhead introduced himself as Chip, and he introduced his friend as well. We talked for a while, until my dad made me go back inside. A year went by, we met up again, same place, same time. This time we talked...and talked...and walked around together and even shared some french fries. The rest is history. Little did I know, that redhead was to be my future husband and the father of my children.

Years passed and we kept in touch by writing letters about the summers when we were reunited. I was a little snot because I decided to keep my options open, and I wrote the same letter to both rodeo boys. I left the name area blank and would write in Chip or his friend's name and mail them. It was rather ingenious, if I do say so myself. But, I never thought about the fact that they were best friends. They were comparing letters – love letters that were photocopied because the content was the same in both. I was busted, but they never told me. Chip still has those letters to this day. I must say, they are quite a read!

Chip decided to join the Navy at the tender age of 17, and I didn't know a thing about his plans until I received a letter one day at my house when I was 14. He told me about boot camp, and what he was up to, and then he asked if he could call me. I got permission from my father and we began talking on the phone…often. When I turned 15, Chip came home on leave from California and my parents allowed me to go for pizza and a movie. That was one night I will never forget. THE REST IS HISTORY…I have been smitten ever since. We dated from the time I was 15 to age 17.

We did break up once in that time frame, which I WON'T elaborate on. Let's just say it was needed so that we could realize that others didn't make us as happy as we were when we were together. I will say that it wasn't a pretty breakup. I haven't let him live it down yet.

Once we got back together, Chip and I had a long-distance relationship for several years. He spent a lot of time and money coming to Pennsylvania to visit me. Our phone bills were outrageous, and our frustration was at a heightened level constantly. At the tender ages of 17 and 20, we got engaged. He proposed in his little hometown of West Hickory, Pennsylvania, up on the hillside overlooking the town. It was very sweet and quaint. I was a senior in high school and engaged to be married. We wanted to have a long engagement. The distance was tough on us. As any military wife can tell you, it doesn't get easier. It actually gets harder and harder to deal with. Hence, we decided to get married as soon as I turned 18. My 18th birthday was Jan 25th, and we married March 10th of the same year. I was a senior in high school and married to a Navy man. You can imagine how his buddies must have harassed him over that cradle robbing! And you can also let your imagine go wild with the rumors that circulated that were false. I was happy to show them that they were wrong, and that this marriage would indeed last. And that 9 months after our marriage, there was no bundle of joy.

The military makes men and women grow up so fast. Sometimes too fast, I admit. But Chip and I were eager to get married and start our life together. This is where my journey began as a military wife, and it has taken me to where I am today.

Chapter 1

Married and Graduating High School

My Navy man and I got married in March of 1990. I was 18 and he was 21. (I remember my friends were so excited that I married an older man: he could buy beer! They were so thrilled.) Ahh, to be 18 again!

We were planning a long engagement until my father got sick of the lovebirds. He decided that one weekend when Chip was home on leave, we would go to the justice of the peace and get married. We both refused. I wanted a wedding! I was determined to have one! So, my father asked how March sounded. We agreed and started to plan a wedding. (We planned a wedding for approximately 500 guests in 3 months during my senior year in high school!)

Chip was then stationed in Norfolk, Virginia, on a submarine. He was a sonar tech and a diver on the sub. I was fascinated by submarines, and I loved the fact that there were no women on them for me to compete with. (Remember, I was 18!) In chapter 2 I will dive (no pun intended) into the realm of the submarine life and being a submariner's wife. It was crazy, and to this day, I have much respect for submarine wives. You girls deserve a pat on the back. It's not easy being a submariner's wife.

We continued our engagement long distance. He lived in Norfolk, Virginia, and I was still in Kittanning, Pennsylvania. Chip would drive 7 to 8 hours every weekend to see me, talk about the wedding, and plan our life together. He talked this Navy thing up like it was paradise. I was so sold on it; I couldn't wait to get to the Navy base to experience it all. *Moving to foreign lands, meeting interesting people, and seeing the world.* I must say, I couldn't get out of my parents' home fast enough with that enticement. I thought it would be heaven; every day sitting on an island with palm trees and sunshine, drinking from a coconut shell. I even imagined a cute cabana boy refilling my drink. Oh, paradise was not quite as I had imagined it…as we headed to Portsmouth, Virginia. But, before moving, we planned a big wedding, traditional in every way, with some Native American traditions thrown in for good measure. (My dad has Native American heritage, and we have many Indian friends who we honored with the Native American traditions and several ceremonies at our wedding and reception. It was beautiful.) I must add that, being 18, I was the coolest girl in school since it was like a big KEG PARTY to my friends. "Jasa's getting married this weekend and is having a reception in West Kittanning. Were you invited?" was the talk in the hallway. Even my high school teachers were coming to the wedding and reception. (I hoped it wouldn't affect my grades, unless it was in a positive way.) I still have the cookbook that my home-economics teacher gave me as a wedding gift. I hope it was a nice gesture and not a sign that my cooking skills in her class were atrocious.

The night before my wedding, I was serenaded from my window, a memory etched in my mind forever. The song "When I See You Smile" still makes me giddy like a schoolgirl. The wedding day was perfect. I don't remember a lot about the details on my wedding day as it was a lot for an 18 year old to comprehend. No matter how mature I was said to be for my age, I was still an 18-year-old girl in a whirlwind romance. I really wanted to have the wedding before school was out, because I knew most of my best friends were headed off to different colleges, and we were all going our separate ways. We thought, what better time to celebrate our eternal love for each other but with our friends and family before everyone is gone? It was a great evening, the ceremony was perfect, and the reception was also.

We left the morning after the wedding from Pittsburgh International Airport for a flight to Couples Resort in Jamaica. That, too, was pure paradise. Imagine this, a high school senior going into the principal's office to request a week off of school to go to her honeymoon; you know there were some chuckles after that meeting that day. I didn't care. I was in love and now married! We went, and I returned from my honeymoon all tanned, tired, and hair braided like a Jamaican tourist! Now I had to finish up my schoolwork, like a normal 18-year-old student and graduate so I could go to this paradise life as a Navy wife as I was promised. (Paradise, or so I thought). When we returned from our honeymoon, Chip was still in town a few days on leave before he had to return to his submarine in Virginia. That night was the most awkward night of my entire life. I was now married and returning to my parents' house with my husband for the first time. Do we sleep in separate bedrooms? I was only 18 and still in high school. Do we sleep in my bedroom where I still had all of my posters on the walls and my silly teenager décor? Do we sleep in the spare bedroom? We decided to sleep in the spare bedroom, but it took literally hours before we both made our way back there. We were so tired but scared to be in the same bed in my parents' house. We opted for the safest route. We slept in the bed together on top of the covers with our clothes on. And I really don't think either of us slept that soundly that evening. By day two it was a little more comfortable, but we were never comfortable enough to go to bed early. We stayed up as late as we could every night he was still in town after our honeymoon until we couldn't stay awake any longer. We then made that awkward trip down that long hallway to the spare room as husband and wife.

Yes, I was a senior in high school, and NO, NOT PREGNANT! Just foolishly in love. I took my husband to my senior prom with a dress handmade and intricately sequined. Before the prom, I had to go into the principal's office to request permission for Chip to take me to the prom. There was a clause where no one over the age of 20 was permitted to attend the prom without pre-approval by the principal. Thank goodness the principal approved my husband to take me to the prom! That could very well have caused our first fight as husband and wife. What was even funnier was that I was on homecoming court my senior year when I was engaged to be married. Most of the people knew Chip since we had dated for a few years. But, it was a neat thing to have made homecoming court regardless. I was very active in school. I was the President of Student Council, Vice President of SADD and many other groups, which kept me busy my senior year. I decided to graduate with my maiden name instead of my married name not only because most knew me as that, but my maiden name starts with a B, and my married name starts with a S. I had a huge graduating class; I'm no fool! I went with the B and headed down the aisle early into the proceedings.

The night of graduation, we briefly went to a friend's graduation party that evening but left early to pack up my bedroom from my parents' house into rental truck and be on our way as husband and wife…and onto the military life! The very next morning after I graduated high school, we got on the road as early as possible. Here I was 18, married, and leaving home for the first time.

I admit, I cried the whole 7-½ hours to Virginia Beach, Virginia. I had such mixed emotions and cried myself to sleep that day. My husband was so supportive, and he knew I would be okay once we got to our new apartment. It was so true. We pulled into the parking lot and I realized I was a grown up and a married woman. And best of all, I had an apartment to decorate! I felt renewed. (Isn't that therapeutic to many of us? Shopping really cures what ails me.)

I had my moments, which is to be expected. But at age 18, I was already so busy being a wife and grownup, I didn't have much time to look back.

I might add that my biggest fear as a new wife was cooking. I was a good cook, but my first month as a married woman, I learned an important lesson about cooking…When making chocolate chip cookies *DON'T FLIP THEM HALF WAY THROUGH BAKING LIKE YOU WOULD A PANCAKE*! Yes, I did, and no, I haven't lived it down yet! (My mom was a great cook, but I didn't spend much time baking, so how was I to know?) I also learned that it's imperative that when making hard-boiled eggs you place the eggs in the water BEFORE it begins boiling. That too was a mess, and after several attempts, I called home to ask my mom what I was doing wrong that was causing the eggs to explode in the water. Again, I was 18…what did I know?

Chapter 2

Submarine Wife

Well, here is where the journey begins. For those of you who are Navy wives reading this, you will understand what is being said, not said, and even implied in this book! It *is* the "toughest job in the Navy." You see the shirts and mugs everywhere that have the saying, it's funny until you live the life. Then when you pass a shirt that says that or a bumper sticker, you chuckle, and you think to yourself how true it is! I use to think that was crazy, but now I know it to be so true. It didn't get as difficult until we had children, That is when I really discovered that Navy wives deserves so much more respect than they receive on a daily basis. We support our husbands unconditionally, move our household at a drop of a hat, and learn how to have them in and out of our lives in a moment's notice at times. My first Navy experience was when my now husband told me he was a sonar tech and diver on a submarine. I said, "No, really, what do you do in the Navy?"

Submarines…I knew so little about them, but soon I would discover that they would become my whole life.

My first trip to see a submarine was at the sub base in Norfolk, Virginia. My future husband took me to his submarine to give me a tour. I walked down the pier with him in amazement of this bullet-shaped boat in the water. I was corrected so many times calling it a ship. It is not a ship, it is a boat. How amazing that over 100 men were down inside that boat working away and living in that mass of metal for months at a time. I was fascinated and scared. It takes a special man to be on a submarine, I came to find out – either a very intelligent man or a really weird one, Thank God, my now-husband fits into the first group. I have since met many that fit into the second.

My fiancé got approval for me to go down on the sub, but I didn't realize I was going down stairs that were STRAIGHT DOWN! I knew it would be stairs but not straight down. This was a feat in itself, I tell you. If you have been on a submarine, you understand completely. I proceeded down the stairs and looked down below me. Oh great! There were men down there, and I had a skirt on! It would have been really nice if my dear fiancé had warned me to not wear a skirt. Now, the whole sub got to know me, and my Victoria's Secrets were no secret. I was so embarrassed. I learned a good lesson, and I tell every submarine wife to never wear skirts or dresses on a submarine. In the same note, I recommend to never wear a skirt on a pier for homecomings either. That has been interesting for photos that I have seen of friends with their SKIRT blowing in the breeze. Save your skirts for events off piers and you will avoid a lot of "situations" mentioned above. Trust me, you think it won't happen to you, but inevitably it will.

I did have the *honor* of attending a "dependant's cruise" aboard a sub in Virginia just before I married. A dependant cruise is where the submarine will take wives or other family members out for a full day aboard the sub to experience what our husbands do on a daily basis when out to sea. The sub actually goes out and under the water for several hours. Several hours of sick puking women, I might add. All I got from the experience was the following: I was sicker than a dog from the rocking of the boat while it was on the surface, not once it submerged, and I was so hungry after being served hard brownies, "bug juice," and food that didn't even resemble its name, that I wanted dry land! Why can't they call burgers by their name? Instead they call them sliders. I have been told because they slide right through you. You will never catch me drinking "bug juice" and eating "sliders" in a submarine. Plus, I knew I never wanted to sleep on any mattress that came off of those subs; they were wafer thin and disgusting. I think sleeping in the torpedo room was much cleaner! (Okay, it is a little more frightening to be sleeping in a room with torpedos, but it was torpedoes or bedbugs.) I feared bedbugs more than the torpedoes, so I opted for the torpedo room. They actually had cot areas under the torpedo storage areas for additional sleeping.

Even though I had been on a sub several times before this event, to actually go underway for the day was an amazing adventure. There were so many procedural things that happened on the sub that the guys performed with ease, but to the rest of us, it all looked so foreign. There were the maneuvers they did while we were underwater. Being able to look out the periscope was a lot harder than it seems. It also surprised me how these men would run through the halls and slide down the stairs never losing their balance. Meanwhile, I was rocking wall-to-wall and ready to vomit at any second. Walking on a sub when it is still on the water is a learned skill. Not one that I had or would ever come to learn. We all posed for pictures at the periscope, like tourists. Being only 5 foot tall, I was at a disadvantage to even be able to see out of the periscope, so they all showed me how I could stand on the metal "step stool" that surrounded the periscope. It was the highlight of the day out to sea for all of the dependants. I still show people that picture to this day. But, I have always teased my husband that he ever has the chance for another dependant's cruise, he'd better find another dependant!

My husband was a sonar tech at the time, so I was lucky enough to spend the afternoon in the "Sonar Shack" and listen and watch monitors/screens all afternoon. They had some great sounds to entertain us like whales, shrimp, and fish of some sort that was surreal. The rest to me it was a lot of little buttons, but they know what every one is for. The guys in sonar had a great job during missions, and it is a fascinating job! My first question in sonar was, "Why do you have rolls of toilet paper hanging in this room?"(And, did I *really* want to know?) They explained that they use the toilet paper to wipe the black markings left from the black pencil they use to mark on the monitors. That was a relief! I knew the subs were basic and no frills, but my fear of what that toilet paper was for was more than I want to even elaborate on paper.

Sonar was confined space, dark and quiet. I would surely fall asleep if I were in that room for hours. The men assured me that rarely happens, but I still wonder. While in the sonar shack, the sub began to do maneuvers and I think the men were showing off, because as the sub began to tilt to one side, the sonar tech's coffee cups began to slide down the table they were sitting at. Without even a bat of an eye, they all simultaneously put their hands out to catch the sliding coffee cups in their grips. Their eyes never left the screen, and not a coffee cup left the table. (Contrary to what the wives' coffee cups ended up doing! Yes, we lost many cups of coffee that afternoon to their amusement.)

I can't forget the time I was walking through the long, narrow hallway on the sub and bumped into the belly of a rather large sailor. I had my back to one wall, sucking in my belly to give him more room; he had his back to the other wall. We still bumped bellies, not appealing! But, that's a submarine for you, too close for comfort and not much comfort anyway! The rest of the dependants' cruise was a bit of a blur to me since I had to take a motion sickness pill and retreated to a "rack" to sleep off my nausea. (There, I was joined by a dozen other women.)

The submariners have a tough job, and there is not a lot of access to ports on some subs. They deserve respect for what they do, because not many could go under the water for months like they do with ease. Granted, some break under the pressure, but this day and age of technology makes it so much easier!

When my husband was in submarines, there was no email; there were only "family grams." What a joke those were! (Those of you who have been in the Navy for a long time remember the days when that was the ONLY form of communication for submariners.) In the next chapter I will elaborate on the *art* of writing a family gram. (Notice the sarcasm yet?)

Chapter 3

Communication with Home

Family Grams

Family grams have a good intention, don't get me
wrong...but prior to email that was all we had to contact our
husbands besides sending packages out and hoping to hear
from them when they were in port. So, for those instances, they
served their purpose as a morale booster.

On subs, you may not be able to send and receive packages.
You also may not be able to talk to your husbands for many
months at a time, and they may not pull into ports. At these
times, family grams become your only source of one-way
communication.

I thought I could deal with that and got excited to have 8-10
of them to send to my husband while he was deployed. That is,
until I read the directions. Here is a sample:

Each crew member may receive 8 family grams a
patrol. Each family gram can contain up to 50 words.
Punctuation does not affect the 50-word limit, so use
it liberally to improve the clarity of the message. Any
code, riddle or off-beat terms will necessitate
returning of the family gram to the sender for
correction prior to transmission. Any questions you

may have concerning family grams should be directed
to the off crew office at XXX-XXXX.

A family gram is generally expected to be good news. They
are sent much faster if they are clear and don't, in themselves,
create questions. A statement such as, "John's operation was a
success," requires that the crew check to see that your husband
knew that a operation was scheduled and that he was expecting
this news. Don't slow down the good news. Keep it simple.
Keep it clear. Keep itclean and don't get too personal, as it will
travel through many hands before reaching your sailor's hands.

Okay, do I even need to elaborate on my issues with family
grams now? Don't say too much, but don't say too little. Be
specific, but not too specific. And please, pretend everything is
great at home and good news even if it isn't. Oh, it's grand to be
a military wife!

Well, my sailor's first deployment came before my period
did. So, we had an issue and no way to discuss it once he left for
Wes Pac. I would either find out I was pregnant while he was
deployed, or find out it was a false alarm. He was on a
submarine at the time and was not going to be in any ports to
call. This was an instance where the family gram was my
lifeline to my spouse for many months. And, being that it could
be our first child on the way, he needed to know something.
But, I knew it wasn't something I could write in a family gram
for every reason listed above.

We devised a plan and hoped the punctuation and words
were sent across the wires correctly to get the answer to him.
The family gram would have two different endings. If I were
pregnant I would end the family gram with: Yes, I love you,
Jasa. If I were NOT pregnant, the family gram would end with:
I love you, Jasa. Now I had to put a lot of faith in the United

States Navy men and women to get this message to my husband, and get it wired there correctly. To be sure, every family gram for deployment I would continue to end the same way to be sure he got the message. The message ended up reading: I love you, Jasa. I was not pregnant! Thank goodness since I was still too young!

Another funny thing that happened was with a friend of ours. He was also a submariner and had the lovely family grams and no ports to have contact for many months. He gave me some family grams to send him some notes and updates on us and the kids. He was a single, quiet-mannered man. A sweet man, who has always been good to my family and is like a brother to me. Well, to keep him guessing through his deployment, I signed all of his family grams with a different stripper name. They varied from Candy, Jade, Trixie, Saphhire, etc. Now the funniest thing about this is, he is not a womanizer. So, this may have changed the opinion of what some of the guys on his sub thought, and may have started some rumors about his studliness! Everyone has to have some fun once in a while, even if it's only on paper.

The last time I sent family grams to the above mentioned friend, I was sure to send once or twice a month to be sure he had some nice little notes to read. It was like clockwork. My calendar had notations to send a family gram out on certain days. Little did I know, he only received a few of them. The other ones either got lost in translation, read and kept by another person on the boat, or were lost forever in cyberspace. This sailor has since returned from another six-month deployment and informed me that yet again he failed to receive all of the family grams I had sent to him while he was underway. Out of ten family grams, he only received one.

Family grams become a bit of a power struggle on subs when that's the only means of communication. The struggle is usually between the wife and the mother-in-law. Luckily for me, my husband's mother is very laid back and did great with allowing me to take over where she left off with her oldest son. I am so blessed to have wonderful, patient in-laws who treat me more like a daughter than a daughter-in law, so we didn't have that issue. But so many times I hear that the women "fight" for the family grams. I have even heard wives fib about the number of family grams allowed to be sent just so the mother-in-law thinks it's a lower number than it is. This I don't suggest, as it will inevitably come back to bite you in the butt someday. May not be now, it may be years from now. Either way, it would be an ugly situation when it appeared. That's one family dinner I don't want to be at!

Email

Wow! When the day of email came into play with the U.S. Navy, it was a dream come true. In addition to those pesky family grams, we could now email our husbands off and on.

On surface ships, the email is more readily available, but I have been told that for any reason, and for many reasons, it can be shut down at a moment's notice. That becomes very frustrating for those wives, husbands, and others who are awaiting a returned email from a loved one who promised to email back. First thing, don't promise emails or any forms of communications. Those are always luxuries, can be taken away within seconds, and may not be returned indefinitely. Ask your sailor to please remember that you are sitting at home checking your email between every task you do in your daily routine in hopes of an email. This is why it is better to be happy about an email when you get it but not expect them. I have talked to so many spouses who were upset that they didn't get an email returned when they were promised one. I urge you to take every email as a benefit and it will make the days with no contact much more tolerable.

Web Cams

Another fun part about today's military is web cams! My husband and I were separated coast to coast while he was in Flight School in Pensacola, Florida. Our children were really missing Daddy a lot, and the plane trips from Florida to California weren't conducive to our wallets. So web cams became our family visitations. We visited via web cam for about 7 months.

Granted, your first thought of web cams are for a more "adult nature" and yes, many have been used for that form of enjoyment. Don't think I didn't think about it. Gotta love technology! Seriously, my kids really needed Daddy, and the web cam was a lifesaver. After school, we would sign on to the web cam and they could tell Daddy what happened at school, or preschool, and actually see the reaction and smile on his face. Every night at 9 p.m. we would all sign onto the web cam, so they could say goodnight to Daddy, and he could tell them he loved them. It made the months go by so much easier, and the kids felt connected to their dad more than on the phone. I strongly suggest purchasing web cams for separations or deployments that are land based. I even had my husband read books to my youngest when she was missing her daddy. When she was sad and missing her daddy, she would go out to the computer monitor and wait for Daddy. At merely 2 years old, her security was that Daddy would appear at the monitor, and everything would be all right again.

I was even told of one Daddy who missed his family so much that he decided to install a web cam in his house so that when they would turn the connection on, he could watch his family's day-to-day activities. It helped him feel like he was there and involved with the family. He felt as if he wasn't missing out on everything, including the children's arguments, pillow fights, and even when they were doing their homework. That seems a little odd, but we often forget that it is hard for the spouses to be without us, too! We get so busy being the Mommy and the Daddy and keeping things going at the home front that sometimes we forget how lonely our husbands are without us. Their days seems longer and more drawn out than ours as we are running errands and cooking and cleaning and working. A lot of times we forget how much they miss the day-to-day hustle and bustle. Be sure to make time out of your busy schedule for your sailor with some form of communication when possible. It will make him feel included even though he is far away.

Chapter 4

First Deployment and First Wes Pac

My first deployment as a sailor's wife was rather unconventional, as I was still in high school...yet married! So, the first deployment that is memorable to me came as a shock to me as well. I was in my senior year in high school, I was married, and my husband was deployed far away. I was too busy finishing school to understand much about deployments at the time. I was busy doing homework and planning for prom and graduation. We had a long-distance relationship for several years, so I was use to living states away. He deployed and called me often. We loved being able to talk for hours upon end – until the phone bill arrived! We spent more on one phone bill than he made on a paycheck. This was not a good start to married life. We started to schedule days when he would call and days when he would not. But, it never failed, he would call on the off day to tell me he missed me, and that five-minute phone call would wind up being hours. My husband was also a Navy diver, in addition to being a sonar technician. When his sub was in the dry docks, he "rode" many submarines to do "dive stuff" with them. (As you will be able to tell throughout this book, I am unversed in the Navy terminology and I am proud of it. This has been an asset to my marriage. I will explain in Chapter 6. We have always separated our home life from our military life.)

One of my most memorable early deployments was when we were living in Virginia Beach. My husband's submarine was in the dry docks. He had been called to be a rider on another submarine that was not in the dry docks. They needed a diver to ride their sub for a 3-month deployment. That would have been fine, but they also were only giving him 3 -hours notice. Yes, 3-HOURS notice.

My sailor called me at work in the middle of an employee meeting and told me to please come home right away because he was deploying in 3 hours for 3 months. I was in shock! I rushed home to find his best friend there as well. He had called his wife with the same shocking news. She was on her way over to our apartment also. They stayed in the living room and spent time together, and we spent some "alone time" together in our room to last 3 months or more. And I cried and cried and cried. Mentally, I was not prepared to be without him for 3 months yet. I was a new military wife without my family for the first time. I was not ready to be alone in this strange town. Yet, I knew my job as a Navy wife was to be strong and resilient. We didn't have much time together by the time I got back from work, and Chip got his bags packed for the deployment. We had to get them to the pier.

The four of us made our way down the pier. Most of the time when the four of us were together, it was good times. The four of us had taken weekend trips to Nags Head, North Carolina, and to many beach get-togethers. This was the first time the four of us had been together without a smile to share. It was very bittersweet. Hand in hand, tears streaming down my face and down his friend's wife's face as well. We walked with gloomy, slumped posture, feeling like we had both lost our best friends. Those men were our world.

The time had arrived, and we said our goodbyes. The men went to the submarine, walking down the long pier. They waved goodbye and started down the ladder. It was as if everything was in slow motion. Step by step, it hurt my heart more and more to see him going farther away from me, knowing I would long for him for 3 long months. I couldn't handle it, so I turned around to leave, only to hear, "Jasa! Wait!"

I thought, *Lord, please don't let him come back for another kiss; I can't say goodbye again.* He was running to me with his sea bag in hand. Instantly, I thought he forgot something or that his sea bag wouldn't fit on the sub, and I needed to take it back home with me. It was neither. He caught up to me and said, "They don't need us now. They have enough divers."

All of a sudden, I was ticked off! "What? You aren't going to sea now?"

He gleamed back at me and said, "No, baby, I'm going home with you." He was smiling ear to ear, and expected me to return the same delight.

In horror, I said, "The hell you are! I am an emotional wreck. I prepared for a 3-month deployment in mere hours. I am now mentally prepared for you to go. You better tell them they are taking you!"

He lost all emotion in his face. I could tell he was horrified. The coloring faded from his face and his jovial smile turned into a puzzled fear. I explained to him that I was indeed happy that he was coming home with me, but emotionally I had already said goodbye and was preparing myself to deal with the detachment from him. He wasn't hurt after I explained the reasoning behind my "uncalled for" outburst. Yet, at that moment I knew...*I am officially a military wife.* I mentally prepared myself and had started to shut down my emotions once he stepped foot on the sub. I couldn't turn it back on so fast. After telling several military friends this story, they assured me that I was completely normal with my reaction and that it's a cycle we military wives go through, just not normally in such a condensed period of time. From that time on, I was ready for anything. Any call, day or night.

My only rule was: if you prepare me for your deployment, you better go. Even if they cancel it.

Humor Me

Humor me, call home at lunch
Do you have time for me today?
Humor me, come home at lunch,
So we can cuddle and play
Too many days you are gone; too many days out to sea.
When you are gone 6 long months, do you remember me?
Places you go. Things you do. Foods you want to try.
I sit at home and wait for your call, and often times I cry.
This lonely house, this lonely bed.
The funny things you missed that the kids have said.
It's hard on you, this I know to be true.
Your days are lonely with out us, too.
So, humor me, and call home at lunch
And make time for me today.
For tomorrow you may be called to war
And I will be left alone to pray.

~ Jasa Shaw 2004 ~

A Sailor's Wife

A sailor's wife has a burden to carry,
Deployed all the time is the man she chose to marry,
She holds her head high and is always strong,
No matter what catastrophe may come along.
We stick together as military wives.
We share a common bond the rest of our lives.
Some days we laugh,
Some days we cry,
Some times the days slowly creep by.
The months will pass
He will be home at last
The family unit will be united and strong,
But we never know for how long.
Enjoy each day, month and more
For tomorrow we don't know what is in store.

~ Jasa Shaw 2004 ~

Chapter 5

Submarine Life

The actual definition for submarines is: a submergible warship that usually carries torpedoes. That is a pretty vague definition for such a remarkable boat. (And if you call it a ship, be ready to be corrected.) It takes a special man to be a submariner. I have only met two types of men on submarines:

1. "Not so normal" men, and
2. Highly intelligent men.

Thank goodness my husband fits into the second category.

In this chapter I will be discussing submarine life from a wife's point of view. Please remember that I am referring to my personal experiences, and that they pertain to life on a Fast Attack submarine, as I have never stepped foot on any of the others in my 14+ years as a military wife. These Submarine Crew members live inside a pressure hull filled with the machinery required to keep them alive and allow the ship to function. They must make do with the cramped spaces between the machines, with very little privacy for many months at a time. The submariner's day lasts 18 hours: three 6-hour watch cycles, 1 on and 2 off. He stands a duty watch, then has the next 12 hours for everything else: repair and maintenance tasks, study, relaxation, eating, and sleeping. Then it's back to the duty watch again.

I am all for equal rights and women's rights, but I still cannot see the place for a woman on a submarine. The space is so limited. For example, berthing (sleeping area on the sub) is the personal space for the crew on a nuclear-powered submarine to sleep in. It is extremely tight, and it is similar to a room full of bunk beds across every wall available in the room. The bins underneath the racks represent the only space a sailor has to store his clothing and other personal items for the duration of a deployment. It is a very shallow space and is so small that the men search for "hiding places" for their additional items underway. Often on a fast attack subs, there is not enough room for the men to even have their own bunks! This is where it gets bizarre. The crowding can be so great that up to three men may "hot bunk," or share two bunks between them, so that when one is on duty, another is asleep. This is not the most sanitary procedure around. Imagine you are underway with a co-worker who has body odor. (There are known to be some men that decide on deployment they are on a break from showering. This is hard to believe, but I have heard of men not showering for weeks at a time.) Then imagine this man sleeping in the bunk before you, even with clean sheets.... aroma doesn't dissipate so fast in a confined room such as berthing. I have nothing else to elaborate on that situation. But, a stinky man in a submarine for 6 months is not the man you would like to have a hot rack with.

The food on a sub is a whole different story. Granted, I mentioned the brick-like brownies, but I failed to mention the shrimp dinners, and some of the benefits of submarine food. Submarines are known to have some of the best cooks in the Navy onboard. Food for the crew is the bulkiest commodity in a submarine and becomes the limiting factor for deployment duration more often than not. Fresh food lasts about two weeks, then it is canned, dried, and frozen food for the rest of the trip. When a submarine leaves for a deployment, food fills literally every available corner. They have been known to have some wonderful meals aboard submarines, and I have never watched anyone leave a submarine mess deck hungry. There are some wonderful cooks on submarines, and the cooks are the ones you want to befriend. They can feed you well or leave you hungry. Don't screw over the cook. Our son used to think it was such a special treat to go visit daddy on his sub and have lunch or dinner. At the tender age of 2, our son Cody use to say, "Can we go see Daddy, so I can have some bug juice?" Bug juice is the term used for juice on a submarine. It is the sugary, Navy-issued Kool-Aid equivalent. It doubles up as a great super strength toilet cleaner. No, I am not joking. It served a double purpose on the submarine. Fourteen years married I can honestly say I have never tasted bug juice. The stories I have heard about its uses were enough for me to opt for a different beverage or take bottled water when I visited. Eating takes place in the crew's mess. Everyone eats in the same room. The mess deck also is virtually the only common space aboard a submarine for training and study, and it is where off-duty sailors can unwind by watching videotapes or playing video games. This is also the area where everything takes place including ceremonies and awards. It's all and all a multi-purpose room.

They have some great meals and meal nights underway. They even have special treats of ice cream. After being out to sea for a period of time, you begin to notice treats coming out of the woodwork on board. Candy, Cup o'soup, beef jerky and the like become a wanted commodity of supply and demand.

There is little ability to work out on a fast-attack submarine while it is underway. The cramped spaces aboard a nuclear-powered submarine make it difficult to stay in shape during lengthy patrols. Sometimes there is a stationary bike or two crammed into any available space. But, that's about the extent of what they can have onboard due to space constraints. Some men complain that the good food and lack of exercise equipment on the subs make for a lot of weight gain during deployments, which leads to another issue: Don't plan to get sick while underway.

Don't plan on getting sick underway. The doc's office on the sub is the size of an airplane restroom. And, no I am not being facetious. I am being honest. The medical room isn't large enough for more than one patient at a time, and there is barely room for the boat's doc to tend to you in the same room. Can you imagine a woman in this tiny room that is not very private and not very comfortable? We women have more medical issues than men. We have to worry about pregnancy, miscarriage, cysts, cramps and more. Now that makes me wonder what the pregnancy rate would climb to onboard a submarine with women onboard. Those confined spaces…I can't imagine the changes that would need to be done to make a submarine unisex. It would have to be a different submarine all together. (And more importantly, with all those space constraints, where would we put our shoes?)

Chapter 6

The Benefit of Separating Work and Personal Life

There are so many advantages to separating work life from home life, especially for the military families.

We have tried living both ways, and both of us agree that separating the two is much more relaxing and much less stressful for us. This is our personal opinion and everyone may not agree. A good example would be those times in everyone's life when they have disagreements with neighbors or friends. When these disagreements happen, whom does it affect? You and the neighbor, or you and the friend. When you are in a military community and have a disagreement, who does it affect? You and the neighbor and the neighbor's husband and your husband. Then it can go on to a bevy of people after that including the housing office, the housing manager, your husband's superiors, your husband's squadron, unit, etc. It's not worth the drama. And in a lot of military housings, there is a lot of drama.

I lived in military housing for the first time in 1999. I agreed to this because this housing was fabulous! They were brand new renovations, not base housing, but government-owned housing in San Diego. They were detached homes at the beach. I couldn't go wrong. I realized how much I still was determined to separate my work life and personal life when I chose the house for our family. The house I chose was on a cul-de-sac away from all the other government houses, and we had civilian neighbors to our left. There were military neighbors below our house, but their house even faced a different street, so we didn't really ever see each other. We were in the neighborhood but out of the development that was similar to a subdivision. I am a very social person, so I wasn't choosing that house to avoid people. I just didn't want to be in the "drama" of military living. And it ended up that it was a good choice. The house was great; the neighbors were great. Everything was great until our sticker changed on our car. Non- Military people always look puzzled when I tell them this story, but I'm sure if you are military or prior military, you read this and you are nodding your head, fully understanding the situation ahead.

My husband was enlisted for 13 years as a submariner on fast-attack submarines; He was a sonar technician and a diver onboard them as I mentioned in prior chapters. He began to apply for an officer program when we decided we were going to stay in and make it a career. He applied for the program a few times. He wasn't selected. One year he was chosen as an alternate, but he still wasn't brought active as an alternate. The final year we decided to try for the Officer Program was also the last year he physically could apply for it due to his age. (It makes him sound so ancient, but he wasn't. But, they had an age limit.) If he was not accepted into the program this last time, we wouldn't stay in. A lot in our life would begin to change. At the last chance, he was accepted! It was a day I won't forget. The fear of the "outside world" could wait a little longer as my husband would now get his commission. I didn't stop to think how this would affect my family or myself. I thought things would be the same as they were; he would just be an officer and make more money. Well, everything changed. Yes, for the better but with some realizations. We had moved to housing in Pacific Beach, California. He was finishing up schooling at San Diego State University, and his military time was at USD Campus. We were pregnant with baby number two (McKenna Lynne) when he was finishing up his college. That was a whole different challenge financially for us. We moved to the housing to be able to afford our new addition, as well as college. We were paid as enlisted, but were sending Chip to school full time. We had to pay tuition and books out of paychecks. Hence, we acquired some hefty student loans. But in the end, it was so worth it. To make a long story short, we moved to housing as a cost savings during the transition time when our expenses with college were heightened.

As you know, each vehicle that is military has the ever so lovely military sticker on the window. We all know (for those who don't, I will explain in detail) that the red sticker means you are an enlisted service member. The blue sticker means you are an officer service member. There are other colors for retired and for nonmilitary government employees, etc. I came from 13 years married to an enlisted submariner. Yet, on submarines they were a very tight-knit community where there wasn't a large separation between the two, except at work. When we were at social functions or away from work, it was very laid back and officers and enlisted were social. It wasn't uncomfortable by any means.

On one particular day, I took McKenna and Cody to the park. The park was a neighborhood park down the street where the majority of the military housing was located. I was playing in the sand with the kids when I decided to talk to another mom who was there with her child. We chatted for a few minutes and we were getting along great. I was happy to have someone to talk to while the kids played together. I had several friends in the neighborhood already who knew my situation and Chip's and seemed to be ok with the change we were embarking upon. This young mom asked me where I lived. I said, "I am the only military home on Pico Way." Her response to this day still bothers me. She said, "Oh, the one with the blue sticker?" I stepped back and was in shock. The blue sticker… people had already noticed the blue sticker. I finally came back out of shock and disbelief and told her that no, my house did not have a blue sticker but, yes, my car did. And I asked her if that was a problem. She was very frank to tell me and said, "Well, you aren't suppose to be over here with us."

I told her, "Well, this is where I live and this is where I chose to be." At that point, this was not a friend I wanted to make. I asked her how she knew I had a blue sticker, and she told me her neighbor told her. I knew right then and there that the last 11 years that I chose to separate work from home life, I had made the correct choice. Case in point! Did it really matter that I had a blue sticker? Granted, technically I knew the answer to this question, but in that particular situation it wasn't necessary. I have friends in many fields and of many ranks. To me that is irreverent in casual situations as these. What is relevant is the connection or friendship we share. I realized that I was experiencing a prejudice due to my husband's rank, and I wasn't yet prepared for that. It caught me off guard. We were in an outdoor area casually talking. Nothing more. There are many times today that I still don't tell people if my husband is an officer or enlisted. I just say he is on P-3s and I leave it at that. I don't mention it unless it is necessary. This particular situation that I talked about above made me so uncomfortable. From that day until the day we moved to Pensacola for flight school, I always parked my car backwards in the driveway. Was I embarrassed of the blue sticker? On the contrary I was so proud that my husband was enlisted and worked hard to become an officer. Nothing was handed to him; it never has been. I just didn't want to be judged because of it. We were the odd ones in the neighborhood. I just wanted to fit in until we moved. The housing office sent us a letter telling us we needed to move to officer housing within 30 days of his change of status. At that time, the officer housing was a mere two streets away from where we lived. Yet, we were going to have to pack our house and move two streets away. We contacted housing and explained our situation. They still wanted us to move, but we had found out the officer housing was all being renovated and those people were being moved within the next few months also. That meant another move for me! And we were only one year from transferring. We talked and called and wrote letters to housing begging them to let us stay in our lovely home until his transfer. After many letters and calls, they agreed. It was a blessing! We were able to stay until we left for flight school in 2001.

We have always separated our military life before that short stay in government housing, and we have done the same since we left San Diego. When my husband leaves work, he leaves work at work. It has made our family life very stress free and easy going. It's a good idea to have military friends who understand and can relate to deployments, duty days, and military pay. On the flip side, it's nice to have non-military friends who don't talk about the military with every breath and who you can spend time with and forget about work for a while. Even if just for a night.

I suggest having both as both are a benefit for different reasons. Just be patient with your non-military friends. And expect that when you tell them your husband is on a submarine that they will say things like, "I knew a guy once on a submarine named Jack something. Do you know him?" or "You work at NAS? My boss's son works at NAS. His name is _____. He has blond hair and wears a flight suit." These non-military friends are not trying to be funny. They really think being military is like a family. It does feel like a big family, but even

I don't know everyone in my extended family. Just bite your tongue when asked that question, and don't even bother diving deeper to let them know the magnitude of the submarine fleet, coast to coast…or how many thousands of people work on NAS. Just smile politely and let them know you are sorry, but that it doesn't sound familiar. It's a much easier explanation!

Separating work life from home life also comes in handy in the language exchanges. I have talked to friends who live and breathe the military. They are so military minded that they do things like have their children do pushups as punishment in the home and use words commonly known as military lingo in their home life. I have heard phrases that included, "I don't have gouge for that." (Gouge is a word commonly used in the military in reference for having information on an item. To have gouge is to have the details or information.) I have several times been asked, "Where's the head?" I always have the same comment, "On the ship or on the boat. There isn't one in my home." (Head is a word commonly used in lieu of restroom.) If you separate home from work, these phrases won't make it into your house.

And please don't let your sailor come back from a deployment and into your home with a "mouth like a sailor." It happens a lot after deployments. A husband will return and four-letter words seem to flow from his mouth like sand in an hourglass. Don't accept it. If you aren't accepting of it, it will dissipate in no time. If it still isn't going away, start the old-faithful coin in the jar game you use on your little ones who decide to have potty mouths. Just think what a cute new outfit you could earn from the coin/dollar jar after a 6-month deployment? If my husband had that problem, I would implement the dollar jar the minute he returned home and make it prosperous. If you don't want to use the money for an outfit, then give it to your church in offering or to some other good cause. Either way it will curtail the expletives in no time.

I enjoy our military and non-military friends alike. With my military friends, I have found that it's best to delve into their personal lives to find a common bond besides the military. Find something you have in common, so that your conversations can veer from subject to subject and not just rely on the fact that you are both military. Case in point: not all physicians hang out together, nor do they enjoy being around people in the medical field 24 hours a day either. This is true with any profession.

If you go to a church and you are getting ready to transfer, set up a meeting with your pastor or priest. Have them help you research a similar church with similar styles and beliefs in your new area. The sooner you get connected with your church, the faster you will have an active support system in your new area. It helps to have people around who you can trust when you are in a new place. Where better to have trust than in a church. Sometimes for military families, their church family is their only surrogate family to turn to. If you aren't currently going to church, moving to a new area is the perfect time to try a new church. Take a Sunday and go to a different church of your denomination until you find a good fit. There is no "right church;" there is only the "right church for you." We all need and want different things from church. Search out what you may need and want and it will be your first connection to your new area and to people who will be there for you. And it will be a place where you can feel comfortable. You will meet women to talk to, and possibly some will be military. You will also get your children settled quickly into a routine. Military children are especially needy of routines. The routine of going to Sunday school every Sunday and seeing the same children will be a comforting place for them. This is especially true if you transfer during the summer months when school is out of session. Either way, make it a point to find a church before you even get to your new duty station. That will give you a great place to connect with other great people and start the process of settling into your new environment.

Chapter 7

Be a Proud Navy Wife

It is a great thing to be an American; don't ever forget it. Our husbands' risk their lives so that we, our children, and every American citizen out there can live freely. Fly your flag proudly and hold your head up high to show you are proud to be an American and proud to be a Navy wife of an American serviceman.

There is not a day that passes that I neglect to feel pride for being a Military wife. I don't talk about the military a lot, and I do separate my home life from my husband's work job. But that isn't done for anything other than giving our lives a chance to be "normal" whereas the military lifestyle is not conducive to such a thing. I love being a military wife. I am proud of my husband and every military man and woman who serves his or her country. Being an American is an honor that we must not forget. I wear NFO wings on a chain around my neck, and I wear them with pride. I am a proud wife of an American Serviceman. It makes you think about how unique the military is as a whole. What other professions take their men away from their families for six month to one year, and sometimes even longer? There are none that I can think of. I can't think of any that are not voluntary. I know that police officers, firemen, and medical professionals work shift work and that that would be the closest to our lifestyle. Those women have to deal with life at home for days at a time without their husbands, but their husbands are still close to home and accessible. If an emergency arises, they can get to their families if they have to. These professionals are gone mere days – not months, and certainly not years. If they are, it's by choice. I have heard of military fathers receiving messages from Red Cross about emergencies or accidents that involved their wives or children when there is absolutely no way to return them home for a specified amount of time. I know of men who have missed their own parent's funerals due to the war, and have missed weddings of their little sisters and surgeries of their spouses. The distance makes it so much harder than anyone can imagine unless they are military. If an emergency arises, you can't call your spouse first. He can't be there, and most of the time, he isn't accessible. You have to deal with it on your own. For example, my situation at the present is that my husband is deployed. He is at a place where there are no phones in the rooms. There is no way for me to contact him. If an emergency arises while he is there, I will take care of it myself, and then call his squadron overseas so they can get a message to him. It may be days before he finds out what happened. And, that's just a part of the job. I have watched women go through surgeries without their spouses, deliver babies with out any family there, and deal with death alone. But, those are the times that we military wives need to stick together and be there for each other. It's a bond and a connection that only we military wives understand. It's an unwritten rule to be there for each other. And it never fails, when in need… a military wife will be there to help you out! And, if her husband isn't deployed, most likely she will volunteer him as well.

I recently had a super couple come to my aid to put a kitchen table together. I had asked a couple people to help me put the table together, and everyone gave me different reasons why they couldn't do it, or why their husbands couldn't help. Or when I mentioned it, they just changed the subject like they didn't even hear my plea for help. I gave up asking and decided I would tackle it little by little each night and just make it a long-term project for myself. I didn't realize I was asking the wrong people. Most people don't really realize how difficult it is when your spouse is deployed. They say they understand or can relate, but they can't. I don't hold that against anyone. Unless you are military, you really can't understand and I don't expect you to. It's a crazy lifestyle and I don't think it's for everyone.

Back to the story – I stopped asking people and just decided to leave it where it was, and I wasn't going to ask anyone else to help me put it together. Then one Sunday morning at church, one my close neighbors/friends and I were talking and I mentioned the table that I got on base because it was a great price. I was just laughing about the size of the box. The box was so small and thin, and I knew the table was large when put together. That meant one thing…lots of parts! So, I joked about it and said it would be waiting for Chip when he returned home from deployment. I never even asked her to help, yet this military family didn't hesitate to say, " I will help you put it together. Is tonight okay?"

I was so touched. I said, "Are you serious?"

She said, "Absolutely! I will have my husband come over to help, too."

I was almost in tears. I didn't expect anyone to help me put such a horrendous project together. I especially didn't expect them to do it the same day. They came over and spent the next few hours putting this table together for me, asking nothing in return. And do you know why? Because military people take care of each other when in need. They are a wonderful and giving military family with four children in their home, and they took time out of their day to help me because they knew my husband was deployed. I couldn't thank them enough. I will never be able to tell them how much they meant to me by that small token of kindness. The same family went through a rough deployment a while back and the husband was left to take care of the children while the wife deployed. I use to make double dinners to send over to them as I knew it was a crazy time. Dinners are a great thing to help out military when the spouse is deployed. Especially when the spouse is the female in the household. It's very easy to double up a recipe and it really helps a single dad alleviate one stress for the day. Military families really watch out for each other. Many times we are the only ones who think of things like dinners, mowing the grass, and the challenges of putting things together.

My husband and I met while the song "Proud To Be An American" was playing in the background. It became our song, and hearing it brings back nostalgic memories. But when I hear that song, I always cry. It has nothing to do with it being our song. It has all to do with the words to the song. The song starts to a phrase referring to the fact that if everything were gone tomorrow that he had worked for all of his life, and he had to start over with only his children and his wife he would still be happy to be living in a land that stands for Freedom. He is and I am proud to be an American and proud to be free. And the song rings so true that it always touches me and brings me to tears. I love America to the point of tears. Every American should love this country with the same zest, honor and pride. We are lucky to live in America and lucky to have the freedoms that we have. Don't take them for granted. Don't forget about the men and women who gave their lives to give us the freedom we have today.

Chapter 8

If It's Going to Happen, It's Going to Happen When He's Deployed

The title of this chapter speaks for itself. I could write an entire book on the trials and tribulations that occur when your spouse is deployed. But, I am going to condense it to a few recent experiences that are my most memorable.

I am sure many of you have times during deployments when things happen that would not normally occur. These are often occurrences that you would never even think to make preparations for before your spouse deploys. That is my life in a nutshell, too. We are such a strong group of women, and we deserve every bit of credit we get for the patience and perseverance we have. I have seen many of you changing a tire for a first time, mowing your yards, edging your yard, and so much more.

I went through my first storm alone when my husband was on one of his first short deployments of our married life once I moved to Virginia Beach with him. We lived in these cute apartments with a great waterway behind them. This was a great, relaxing area until the first storm blew through. Chip was out to sea, and I was home alone. This was before we had children. There was a hurricane. The winds were getting so strong that things were blowing past my sliding glass doors, and the water was rising. I didn't know what I should do, so if all else fails…call Mom! I called Mom and she told me to be calm and get in the closet. I didn't know what to take with me. This was my first-ever storm alone. I grabbed my phone, a flashlight, and the Bible. This is what I went in the closet with. My mom was on the phone, and she was puzzled at my choice of items for safety. She knew the flashlight was not for the electricity being out, it was merely for me to be able to read the Bible while I was locked in the closet for safety. Hey, in times of crisis, we all need different things for our serenity. Mine was my Bible. The storm blew by, along with patio chairs, tables, and debris. It got calmer, the wind stopped howling, and I came out of my closet and resumed my day. I survived my first test as a Navy wife.

When we moved to San Diego, California, I experienced my first earthquake while Chip was gone as well. This was in 1993. The quake caught me off guard in our town home. I didn't recognize it as a quake until it was over. My first thought was that someone was shaking my house via my porch and trying to get in. Granted, we lived on the second floor, but that didn't cross my mind at that moment. And as I mentioned, Chip was gone, but not on a deployment this time. He was at the pizza shop picking up dinner! To me, at that moment, that was just as bad. After living in California a few years, the earthquakes and aftershocks became second nature. We both began to sleep through them with no problems. The only time I can remember a quake waking me up was a big one that messed up Los Angeles. And the only reason it woke me up was because it caused me to fall off of the couch. If it hadn't been for that, I would have slept through that one, too. They became a form of entertainment, the rolling of the earthquakes at weird hours of the day.

The most recent traumatic event was in 2004 living in Jacksonville, Florida. My husband was deploying to meet his squadron that was already deployed. He was missing half of the deployment, and I felt so lucky to have him here longer. Half out of love, half because he had a lot more to do on his honey-do list. Nonetheless, I was glad he was not deployed. Hurricane season arrived. We had lived in Florida for two years now and had not really had any big problems with storms. Hurricanes Charley, Frances and Ivan hit the state over a span of five weeks this summer, causing billions of dollars of damage and more than 60 deaths. And as I write this chapter, we are expecting Jeanne to hit, and two more are on their way after her. When the news reporters started talking about Hurricane Charley, we listened but didn't really know what we needed to do to prepare. The news said that shops were out of water, flashlights, batteries, and generators. That sounded absurd to me. I thought where we lived we didn't need all of those things. I didn't prepare. Charley came and went and it was rather uneventful. Shortly after Hurricane Charley didn't affect us, Hurricane Francis tore through here like nothing I have ever seen. Chip was home for the Sunday that Francis made landfall on the coast area. His flight was to leave on Labor Day, the next day. Before the storm arrived, we went to church and spent time with our church family before sending Chip off to deployment. The storm was beginning to come onshore. The winds were picking up, and the trees were swaying. We ate and went home to find our electricity was out and huge tree limbs were broken in our front yard. Chip hadn't packed for deployment yet, so we rushed around to get his items packed up while we still had daylight. We really thought we had seen the worst of it, and little did we know that the worst was yet to come. The trees swayed, branches snapped, and shingles were flying through our neighborhood like frisbees. We had to get to bed, but the heat with no electricity was unbearable. The next day we drove Chip to the airport to leave. We still had no electricity, and now no water. There was a threat of contaminated water, so we had to boil water. (Which would be easy to do if we had electricity.) Our contact with the outside world was a radio that my dad had given to me the year before. He told me to keep it, that I might need it. I didn't think I ever would; yet it was heaven sent. I could program it to the TV stations. So, for the next four days we listened to our TV shows and our weather reports that way. The newscasters were on my last nerve. They would continually give us a website address to go to report electricity was out. (Question: How do I sign on to the Internet if I don't have any electricity?) Chip called from overseas to check on us and asked if the electricity was back. By day three I had finally decided I was going to lose it. I needed to get the kids out, get them bathed, and provide them with a good meal. (By day three, we were cooking soup, grilled cheese and more on the barbeque grill.) I tried to find a place on base to get shower; they turned me away. I had a meltdown *over a shower*. The poor gal had to listen to me rant and rave. I talked to her supervisor's supervisors… and they let us use their showers. (Thank goodness!) From there I decided to stop and get gas in the car. I was feeling clean, even after the drama of not being allowed to use the showers at the gym, and I decided to get the car prepared in case we needed to go to Pennsylvania to escape the storm. I stopped on base to get gas, and there was more drama. I was pumping gas, and this gentleman comes over and says to me, "You aren't pumping premium, are you?"

I said, "Yes, I am. Why?"

He went on to tell me that they have signs they are placing on the pumps to let everyone know that the mid- and high-grade gas has water in the lines. He said this ever so casually. I almost didn't believe him until he pointed in front of my car and showed me three other cars that had stalled from pumping the gas. I freaked out again. I had pumped almost ten gallons of water into my tank. My cell phone was dead since I have been without electricity for three days; I needed gas to drive to Pennsylvania to get away from the storm, and now what was I to do? He told me to drive the car around and if it stalled, they would come to get me and fix it. I explained to him that I just begged for a shower, I had no cell phone, my husband was deployed, I had no electricity or water, and my food in my fridge was all spoiled. There was no ice to be had at the stores, so I couldn't even buy lunch meat to keep on ice. *And he's telling me to go for a ride to see if the car is messed up?* This guy was insane. I wasn't going anywhere. So, I pulled the car forward and turned the car off…and cried…and cried…and cried. It sunk in. I had no power, no way to cook in my house, my food was spoiled, the water contaminated possibly, and I was undoubtedly going to get sweaty in my house tonight again and have no way to shower – not to mention, the water in the gas tank and no cell phone charged up for an emergency. The kids were in the back seat and I know they were thinking that Mommy had lost it! But, after that good cry, I was ready to be a military wife again and said the heck with all the problems. I have things to do. I drove over to the gas station shop, gave that gentleman looks that could kill, and went in and got a gas treatment bottle. I stood out there in the rain. (Oh, did I mention it was a downpour from the hurricane? It was raining buckets through this experience.) I read the directions to the treatment and I poured it in my tank. I drove off, sputtering away. I made it home and thought that at least I was at home safe with my kids. If I couldn't make it to Pennsylvania for safety, so be it. I would get to a shelter since I couldn't very well take a car with a tank full of water on a road trip anyway.

Did I mention the tornado warnings in the midst of all of this? Oh yes, of course. Every so often, we had to also run from our electricity-less house into a hotter-than-normal laundry room with a cat litter box. There, we hung out in the dark together. It was during one of those moments, hunkered down in the cat feces aroma laundry room that had no windows, hence no ventilation, that my brother-in-law called to check on us. He is a great brother-in-law. He always calls to check up on us, yet he is in the Air Force himself and gone a lot from his wife and children. He called to see how we were doing. Mind you, my husband hadn't called for a while and I was at my wits end. My brother-in-law, Chad, called and said, "Hey, Jas. I was just calling to see how yinz (Pittsburgh lingo for *"you all"*) are doing."

I said, "Oh, let me tell you how we are doing! ..." And I ever so crankily elaborated on the whole situation. You see, I was stuck in a laundry room with two kids, a cat and again...cat feces aroma with no air. I had all the time in the world to talk, and poor Chad was the lucky/unlucky one to call. He was a very good listener that night, and I thank him for that. I'm sure Chip does, too. The kids didn't say a peep. They were probably thinking that they were stuck in that room with an insane mom. Normally, I am a very strong woman, and I don't break under pressure, but come on! Did you read what all happened in one day to me? That's enough to break even the strongest of women. It was that night that I broke down and called a few friends to see if I could come over if I didn't get electricity back. Finally, I called one friend rather late that night when I got the nerve to call. We went over to sleep there for the night. This is one of the hardest things for me to do. If I have ever asked a friend for a favor, know that I have thought about it and over analyzed it until I was blue in the face. As military wives, this is something we need to be able to do, and I am getting better at it. We need to stick together and help each other out and offer our help to each other. Some may be too shy or embarrassed to ask for help. Some may not like to be a burden to others and won't ask for help. (The latter, that's me.) But, I really love the connection that military families have. The house I stayed at that night was that of a fellow Navy wife whose husband was deployed with the same squadron. The husbands didn't know each other, but we did. Same thing happens when I do ask for help with anything around the home. I seem to find myself calling other military families. They can relate, and they understand. Most of them have been in a similar situation at one time or another. Military families are the closest families in the neighborhoods I have lived it, and they are the ones who seem to borrow things back and forth from each other. We have this bond that we can borrow anything and everything and never feel odd about asking for it. We have borrowed and have had items borrowed from us such as lawnmowers, tools, cars, garbage cans, food of every kind, toilet paper, beds, chairs, and tables. We don't think anything of it. We are there for each other. It's a unique bond that fellow military have. Enjoy it and live it.

As I prepared to finish this chapter, a lot has happened that I had to elaborate a little more. In the past six weeks we have experienced four major hurricanes. Specifically in Florida, we have been affected by Charlie, Francis, Ivan, and Jeanne. Mere weeks after Francis caused so much catastrophic damage, Jeanne showed up and graced us with her presence. I prepared, as everyone else did for this storm. I didn't buy a generator; the cost and lines were outrageous. I figured that a hotel room would be cheaper and safer for me if I had to go that route. I prepared with my water, flashlights, snacks, canned foods, weather radio, chocolate supply, and more. The storm approached, but amidst the preparations I had to drive an hour away to a Pop Warner Football game and pretend there was no hurricane on the way. As I rushed in the car after waiting to hear the latest weather report, I began to get angry with my husband for not being here. (This mix of emotions is normal and can switch at any moment from anger to sadness.) There may be no pivotal reason for the change, but this time there was. The coach asked me what time I was supposed to be there. I was to be there by 10:30. They were leaving for the game at 10:30. It was 10:30, I wasn't late but I was barely on time. But I knew that question meant I was in trouble as was my son. I went from frantically preparing for a storm and football game to mad as heck at my husband and Pop Warner and everyone involved for having a game that day. I got in my car and cried like I hadn't cried for weeks – well, specifically since Hurricane Francis and the parking lot with the water in my tank. I couldn't even drive out of the parking lot I was so mad and upset. My world began to crumble down that day, and it takes a lot to do that. Although, there's always the straw that broke the camels back. The straw that day was when I was single parenting and rushing to a football game while I knew I had a tire that was going flat, I had a storm to prepare for, and I was so happy I even made it to the field at all. I cried most of the trip to the football game, as did my daughter. She sat in her car seat saying, "I wish my daddy was here. He always knows what to do in weather." Yes, I cried more! *Now my 5-year-old thinks I am not competent enough to deal with the weather.* She went on to say, " I remember how my daddy hugs me and throws me up in the air and catches me. I miss that." I needed to pull over by this time, but couldn't for fear of losing track of the line of football parents that were caravanning to the game. I made it to the game and put on my dark glasses and my game face. I got to the field and met up with a friend, a fellow military wife. Her husband was on a short trip as well. I asked how she was doing and, by the look on her face, I knew the answer. At that moment I realized I had someone on my side. She was someone who understood and was going through the same mess of emotions that I was at that moment. We laughed and cried and shared our thoughts. We were both sure our husbands ears were burning as we were discussing the approaching storm as we sat in a field for a football game. We talked about all the things we needed to do alone to prepare for this storm since our husbands were gone, and it confirmed that I was sane after all. We talked and, of course, won the game, and made our way home.

On the way home, I was losing air in my tire due to what I found out later was a broken tire stem. I drove cautiously and couldn't wait to get home. Another (of course) military family offered to follow with me to be sure my tire didn't blow out on the hour-long drive home. We exchanged cell phones numbers and were on our way. A military family to the rescue yet again! We arrived home and began to make final preparations for the incoming storm. We packed up everything from the yard and waited. The storm arrived with zest. It was in full force by Sunday afternoon. The wind began to pick up, and the rain hadn't stopped in several hours. Like clockwork, my electricity was out again with this storm. After the last storm and four days with no electricity, I vowed to make myself ask a friend for a favor and take my kids to air conditioning for the evening. I did just that; I headed to a friend's house. My kids were thrilled as they adore this family and their kids. They were excited to go over there for good reason. They are honest, giving and a God-loving family. They always make me feel welcomed and like family; I thank them for that. We spent the night there and the next day as well. The next day I decided to drive over, feed the cat and assess the damages. I had this odd feeling that I should go over to the house, but the air conditioning and company felt so good, I kept putting it off. I finally came home, brought the kids along, and my friend's boys too. We pulled into my driveway to see the neighbors taking pictures of my house. The photos were for an obvious reason. There was a huge tree limb on my porch and roof. A part of my favorite maple tree had broken off and landed on my house. It was a very large part of the tree that wasn't going to budge easily. I parked the car, got out and just laughed. That's all I could do. One neighbor said she thought my reaction would be to cry, because she knew I adored this beautiful, shade-giving tree. But, in light of other things that had happened to me recently, all I could do was laugh. It was amazing how many friends in my subdivision just pitched in and started hacking away at this monstrous tree. Another neighbor came by to ask if I had a chainsaw. I said I did. He asked me if I also had gas for it. I replied, "It takes gas?"

He said, "Oh, boy. I will handle the chainsaw." I realized I am not the best person to chainsaw the tree. I didn't even know if it took gas. That's a scary thought! The tree was down in about an hour.

I decided to call my fellow football mom/military wife and check on her. To my dismay she had reason to be worried at football as well. The storm decided to flood her house. And her husband wasn't able to fly in before the storm. She had to face Jeanne with her boys alone, too. Her losses were extreme compared to my tree and shingles. She was out of electricity also, but she lived on the water and it flooded her home and caused so much damage that it is going to cost them a lot of time, energy and money to repair and replace tile, wood flooring, and carpeting, which was damaged with muddy, nasty river water. Not to mention, she had shared with me that there were now fish trapped in her backyard from when the water receded. Granted, nature will take its course and the circle of life will be played out with some very happy birds. But, just the thought of what she was going through really hit home. We military wives were left alone to fend for ourselves, and somehow every time we survive. We learn how to deal with devastation and events in our lives alone that most families can't even tackle together. We are a strong bunch of women. We both had a loving family help us out at our time of need, asking nothing in return. This is a rare commodity in this day and age. My son told me that this particular person, one of his football coaches, that was gracious to repair my roof damage said that it was, "An honor to help out knowing that your dad is protecting our country." The rest of my life, that sentence will forever be etched in my heart. There are still people out there that have pride for America and for our men and women of the armed forces. I am lucky to have such good friends and am honored to have those friendships. It is in times of need you find out who your friends really are. It is also at those times you need to reevaluate and realign some of the other friendships.

Two days after Hurricane Jeanne was gone, my sailor called home to ask how things were. Oh, do they never learn? That question leaves things open for so many responses. That question rates about as high as the response of how do I look being "fine." How are things? Let me tell you. In one breath I elaborated the following, "How are things, you ask? Well, the stem in the car tire is split, but not as bad as the tree in the front yard is split and was on our roof, which really isn't too bad considering that the tarp is off the back of the house where the shingles use to be, but that's really not as terrible as the leak on our front porch or of the dryer's shrill buzzer that won't stop unless I unplug it. Did I mention that we lost $600.00 worth of groceries from the storm and lack of electricity? I wasn't sure if I did, but dear, that is how things are. More importantly, how was your day sightseeing?" Dead Silence at the other end of the phone. "Hello, are you there?" I said with anticipation of a speedy response with all the right words. True or not, I needed to hear them at this moment. And as predictable as it is, they were returned to me. They will never know what we go through when they are away on deployment. Words can't even describe the hectic schedules we live to be sure our family's lives are as uninterrupted as possible during that time.

But it still rings true that if it's going to happen…it's going to happen when he's deployed.

Chapter 9

Care Packages

Care packages cheer our sailors up so much when they are deployed. It is a quick way to let them know we support all that they do and that we do miss them. They really look forward to care packaged no matter if they have been in the military 6 months or 16 years. It is always cheerful, and comfort from home.

The following is a detailed list of care package ideas compiled from many years:

- Make goody bags for the single guys in your sailor's division. Fill them with individually wrapped rice crispy treats, candy, beef jerky, or anything below. Adopt a sailor for the deployment, and it will make his day. It's as easy as making two care packages, or adding a mini package in with your sailor's to give to a single guy onboard. It's a good way for your husband to meet some men he wouldn't normally be talking to.

- Always ask local stores to donate items to the sailors. Dentists are always more than happy to donate toothbrushes and floss. You may even have enough to send to single sailors there with your spouse to hand out.

- Homemade cookies take some extra preparation and extra packing, but so worth it for your sailor! If you put them in a Tupperware container or a Zip Loc bag and stick a couple of pieces of bread in them, they will stay fresh (Pringles canisters are a great shipping container to keep them from crumbling, too!)

- Instant Coffee/Flavored Coffee/Hot Chocolate packets.

- Powdered Gatorade-type drinks or Crystal Light type (Send a jug for it, too!)

- Spray a stuffed animal with your perfume. Place it in a sealed bag for shipment. That will keep the scent from getting on everything else, as well as keep the scent contained.

- Record your voice or your children's on a recordable photo frame and send it so he can hear it anytime he wants to. (This could be a little annoying on subs though.)

- Buy plain boxers and paint on hand prints on the back and kisses all over. (I did this one and my hubby STILL has them, but he didn't wear them. He thought they were a cute idea!)

- Make a CD of both of your favorite songs or meaningful songs.

- Videotape his favorite TV shows or sport's games and send the tapes out to him. (This is my husband's favorite package to receive!)

- Send some steamy letters, but leave your name off the bottom in case they are "misplaced." (This comes from experience. It will save you some embarrassment later.)

- Keep a monthly journal. Send it out the first of every month. Write thoughts through the day, funny things that have happened, things that have broken and things you miss about your man. They'll love reading about your days without them.

- Make "coupons" to use when they get home. Some ideas: One half-hour foot massage; One 15-minute back rub, etc... Be creative.

- Wives or girlfriends can send sexy panties. Just be sure to put them in an envelope/bag marked "Private" so he won"t open them in a common area and get embarrassed. Spray perfume on them and place in a plastic baggy to keep the scent.

- Videotape their favorite shows on TV. It's unlikely that they'll get to see their favorites every week with the whole group in the lounge having to agree on something to watch.

- Send a calendar with dates marked, a countdown of days, and little notes here and there to make him smile every day. This also helps him remember important birthdays and anniversaries.

- Send him magazines of his interest or books to read.

- Do you want to mail a cake? If you do, send angel food cake or bunt cakes without frosting. Buy a sealed frosting can and include that with the package for when it arrives. Otherwise during shipping, the frosting will sweat and mold the cake as well as make for a sticky mess once it arrives. Angel food cake is THE BEST cake to ship!

• Want to help him celebrate his birthday in style? Make a party care package and pack up the balloons, party hats, kazoos, party favors, candy, popcorn, gag gifts and have them shipped to your loved one's buddy for a surprise party! This takes planning, so make sure you contact his/her buddy at least a month in advance and ask for their help in making it a special day. The buddy can accept the package, decorate the office, barracks or tent and invite all his/her special buddies to participate in the celebration. Don't forget to include those embarrassing childhood photos! Scan them on your computer and blow them up to full-sized paper. Send them along for wall decorations...

• Have the kids make Daddy homemade cards. They are more special and meaningful. He will love to see the artwork and funny drawings.

• Kool-Aid, pre-sweetened or with Splenda.
•
• Tuna Fish and Crackers.

• Single servings of bagged chips.

• Hard candies are always enjoyed and shared by the men on deployment. Lemon drops/fireballs/gobstoppers/etc.

• Gum/tictacs/etc.

- Cashews/peanuts/pistachios/etc.
- Applesauce, pudding, fruit cups. *Don't forget the plastic spoons!*
- Breakfast bars/granola, and power bars.
- Cereal (dry).
- Pop tarts.
- Instant oatmeal or grits. (That can be made with hot water.)
- Kraft Easy Mac.
- Microwave popcorn.
- Lipton Soup by the packet.
- Playing cards or dominos.
- Sports magazines or whatever interests your spouse.
- Auto Trader magazines are a hit underway; they get passed around more than a dirty magazine!
- Fun stuff for the ones who are boys at heart: Squirt guns/ water balloons/etc.)
- Movies (DVD) for laptops. (Take out of box and put in a sleeve so it takes up less room.)
- Electronic games like BlackJack, slots, etc.
- Send plenty of pictures.
- Send completed school work, so he can feel involved with school.
- Send neighborhood pictures of things that have been changing/trees/new buildings/etc.
- Blow up a balloon, but don't tie it. Holding it closed, use a permanent marker to write a saying or a short letter on the balloon. Deflate it and send with a note that says to blow it up.
- Local paper, local sports page can never get there "late."
- Playstation 2 and Gameboy games.
- Razors, shaving cream.
- Foot powder.

- Shampoo, conditioner.
- Soap or body wash.
- Mouth wash.
- Deodorant (make sure you know what kind he uses).
- Clorox wipes. Just in case the bathroom needs a little extra spot cleaning. Also useful for the bunk area.
- Gel insoles.
- Glade Stick-Ups. These are easy to hang in their racks.
- Blanket.
- Small bottle of Febreeze.
- A small battery-operated fan for their rack.
- Baby wipes are good for fast, easy clean-ups. A small travel pack is best.
- Eye drops, especially for those on the flight deck.
- Send self-addressed stamped envelopes. Often times they don't have the time (or money) to buy stamps and write out envelopes.
- Send him a roll of stamps, so he doesn't have to go to the post office to buy some.
- Calling cards are a nice way to ensure he doesn't break the bank by talking to you on the phone.
- Send padded envelopes and envelopes of different sizes in case he wants to send a gift...
- Sneaker balls – they're like sachets for your shoes.
- A small, battery-operated light with a clip on it is great for hanging in their rack. It's easier to read by than using a flashlight. Check with your sailor. They may have lights in their rack already and wouldn't need additional light.
- Dryer sheets, in a Zip Lock bag. They can use them in their lockers to help things smell fresh, or they can rub them over their clothes before they go out. It's just a nice thing to have.
- Sun block.

- A stain remover stick. (Shout makes a good stick.)
- CD/DVD disk cleaning kit, since the players and the disks will get a lot of use.
- Oodles of Noodles packs.
- Seasonings and spices for foods. (plastic containers)
- Church member? Ask your pastor for tapes of messages to send to your sailor, or tape the services so he doesn't miss a Sunday!

Valentines Day or Anniversary Ideas

I suggest a mix of the following items: ***send very little chocolate, it does not travel well***

- Box of Conversation Hearts (good for all climates).
- Cute pair of boxer shorts.
- Long letter on pretty stationary scented with your perfume.
- An artificial rose (if you are so inclined).
- A lingerie-clad teddy bear!
- Some sexy panties of yours that you are sending just to keep him in the mood!
- New pictures of you for his wallet or his locker.
- Favorite cookies/brownies.
- Rice Crispy Treats. (They travel VERY well.)
- Phone card with a note that he needs to call for a "good time"

Adorable Theme Packages

(It is also a nice idea for Spouses' Club to make packets of these and send to all the men from the Spouses' Club as a little gift to be handed out to all.)

1.
Lifesaver – to remind you that that's what you are.
Gum – to help your unit stick together.
Cotton Ball – to cushion the rough roads.
Paperclip – to hold it all together.
Tootsie Roll – to help you roll with the punches.

2.
The *Cotton Ball* is to remind you that this marriage will be have lots of soft, kind words.
The *Sticker* is to remind you that we will both stick together and help each other out.
The *Penny* is to remind you that you are valuable and special to me.
The *Star* is to remind you, that to me, you shine brighter than the rest.
The *Bandage* is to remind you to heal hurt feelings in your spouse and in yourself.
The *Eraser* is to remind you that everyone makes mistakes and it is okay.
 The *Rope* is to remind you that I will be here for you when you are at the end of yours.
The *Lifesaver* is to remind you that I care and you can come to me when you need someone to talk to.

3.

AN ERASER – so you can make all your problems disappear

A PENNY – so you never have to say you're broke

A MARBLE – in case someone tells you that you've lost yours

A RUBBER BAND – to stretch yourself beyond your limits

A STRING – to tie things together when everything falls apart

A HUG & A KISS – to remind you that someone, somewhere cares about you!!

4.   *A Military Family's Survival Kit*

TOOTHPICK – to remind you to pick out the good in others.

RUBBER BAND – to remind you to be flexible; things may not always go your way, but God will work it out.

PAPERCLIP – for times when your thoughts are scattered and your life seems cluttered, God can help you keep it all together.

BANDAID – to remind you to heal hurt feelings, yours or someone else's.

PENCIL – to remind you to list your blessings every day.

ERASER – to remind you that everyone makes mistakes, and that it is all right to start over.

GUM – to remind you to stick with it and you can accomplish anything.

CANDY HUGS – to remind you that everyone needs a hug each day.

HERBAL TEA BAG – to remind you to take the time to relax each day and remember that you are LOVED!

Chapter 10

Commissary

Where do I begin? I really believe there should be a class you can take when you become a military wife to learn about places on base that you will begin to frequent. I don't mean to learn the hours of operation, or days they are open. That's the least of our worries. For the commissary, it's a commissary etiquette class that is needed. And, like driver's education, this course should be mandatory to be repeated every few years. There are ten simple rules that if not followed can deem fatal. (Not really, but it can be really irritating!)

1) Always go with the aisle traffic. This isn't Winn Dixie or Publix. If you go down an up aisle, patrons and workers will scold you. And sometimes you will be stuck and can't go forward or backwards. Some commissaries actually have arrows on the floors to let you know which way to go up and down the aisles.

2) Don't leave your cart unattended. Cart jackings do occur frequently. (You laugh, until this happens to you when you have an armful of canned goods ready to place in your cart that has now disappeared.) I have lost many carts in the commissary that way. Inevitably it is found an aisle or two over, abandoned. I guess someone else had thought it was his or hers. The funny thing is that they never even take out the extra items they added before the realization!

3) NEVER take more than 15 items in the express lane, even if the cashier waves you in. It's not worth it. It never fails that at that moment a serviceman/woman in uniform will be coming through the line, and they have head of line privileges certain hours of the day.

4) Don't forget to watch your coupons when checking out. I have lost more money that way. Last week is the perfect example: I checked my receipt and noticed a total of $5.00 in coupons that were not accounted for. Double-check your coupons. (And yes, I went back inside and collected my $5.00!)

5) Check out the plants. The commissaries have some of the best greenery around town.

6) Don't forget to tip your baggers. If you do forget to, they will let you know. Most times in several languages, and most times I don't think you would even want to know what was being said!

7) Check the price of your items compared to outside prices. The commissary isn't ALWAYS the best deal. Although they strive to have the most competitive prices, it doesn't always ring true. Be sure to check common items that you use frequently. You may be surprised.

8) Don't expect a certain item to be on the shelf forever. They are forever changing shelves and discontinuing items. And, if you come to the commissary anywhere from three days before a payday until three days after, expect barren shelves. They do stock them full prior to paydays, but everyone seems to shop at those times, too. (For obvious reasons, that's when we have money!) If you can avoid the commissary at the 1st or 15th of the month, please do. Save that money for in-between paydays. The lines are much shorter. I can go straight through the commissary and checkout on off-payday weeks, where on the payday weeks the lines for the checkout are at least 30-40 people deep. Not to mention, the aisles become a place of havoc.

9) Remember where you parked! Some times a commissary trip can start at daylight hours, and end when the sun has gone down. Find something as a marker to remember where you parked. There is nothing worse that after an unbearable grocery shopping excursion to go outside and wander a parking lot in the heat or cold weather and have no idea where your car is. Just take a mental note before you go inside of what door is closest to your car, so you exit the door closest to your car. That will make it easier right there.

10) Drive cautiously when arriving and leaving the commissary. Most commissaries have the highest accident rates on the entire base.

The history of our commissaries is an incredible story. I will attempt to enlighten you without boring you. It began back in 1825, believe it or not. Sales of goods from commissary department stores to military members began in 1825 when Army officers at specified posts were allowed to make purchases, paying at cost. Then by around 1841, an officer could also begin to purchase for members of his immediate family. Commissaries existed to supplement modest military pay and provide wholesome food to those in uniform. The modern concept was legislated in 1866 and actually began in 1867 when officers and enlisted men could make at-cost purchases, and no geographic restrictions were placed upon these sales. The commissary warehouse at every Army post could be a sales location.

The first commissaries stocked a total of only 82 items. The commissary retail function developed and grew, and it roughly paralleled the development of the retail grocery industry. The commissaries' 82-item stock list of 1868 was comparable to the stock assortment carried by a typical civilian dry-goods grocery store at that time. Commissaries kept pace with developments in civilian supermarkets, and today they average well over 11, 000 items. The list of eligible shoppers has also grown. Retirees, first allowed to make commissary purchases in1879, are still allowed to shop. Members of the immediate family (including the widow or widower) of an active-duty or retired military member are eligible shoppers, as are Reservists and members of the National Guard. It is even possible to take non-military in to commissaries these days, but the non-members cannot make purchases. Only the military member is permitted to make purchases. Similarly, as the role of the American military grew larger, commissaries began to spread around the world. The first overseas stores opened in the Philippine Islands and in China in 1899-1900, and were soon followed by commissaries in Panama. Then all the services adopted the Army's concept of commissary sales stores and tailored the concept to needs. The Navy and Marines opened their first commissaries in 1909-1910, and the Air Force inherited its stores from the Army Air Forces in 1947.

By the mid 1970s, each of the services ran its own commissary agency with differing procedures and systems. Surveys consistently place the commissary privilege as one of the military's top non-pay benefits. Many young service members simply could not make ends meet without the price savings provided by the commissaries.

While commissary employee salaries are tax-funded, the patrons themselves pay through a 5-percent surcharge for such things as commissary construction and renovation costs. The surcharge, mandated by Congress and paid by customers on purchases, reduces the cost of building and maintaining modern commissary facilities. Patrons help pay for their commissaries as taxpayers and through the surcharge.

For commissary customers, the level of savings achieved by consistently shopping the commissary rather than commercial grocery stores has risen from 23.2 percent in 1991 to over 30 percent, according to price comparison studies. I can vouch for that easily. Every visit to the commissary reminds me that I need to go there more often. It is truly a cost savings. It is worth the trip. Even if you go only once a month to get your canned items and frozen items, I can promise you will save money. It's not as convenient as the chain grocery stores by our homes, but it's worth the trip because it keeps the wallet fat.

Commissary savings rank, along with medical care, at the top of military members' most valued items of non-pay compensation. Commissaries are also a key part of military retiree compensation. This is a great savings for our retirees.

When customers talk, commissaries listen. The resulting feedback helps store directors and managers determine customer satisfaction and improve their stores. One of the most popular methods for store directors to solicit customer feedback is by talking to a cross section of patrons in small "focus groups." Through this forum, customers can offer opinions, viewpoints and perceptions about their commissary. Focus groups seek a variety of customers reflecting the store's patron demographics, normally seven to twelve people. There are no permanent members – patron participation changes with each meeting, so volunteering to participate is a one-time opportunity. Normally held quarterly, the meeting lasts about an hour, with refreshments and modest tokens of appreciation provided. You can find more out about this program on the commissary website at www.commissaries.com.

Often, focus group participants discuss product selection in the commissary, or they may question a policy. Many new ideas are brought up and implemented because of these focus groups.

Some customers want to speak up to keep certain things exactly the way they are. Others opt for a fresh, new approach. This blend of new and old is what makes this program prosper. Once customers provide this valuable input, store directors proceed with a sense of urgency to develop action plans to help make patrons' "dreams" come true and improve store operations with their help and ideas.

I am also asked all the time why the baggers work for tips, and how that works. A visible part of commissary service worldwide, more than 5,000 baggers work in stores but are not commissary system employees. So, you might ask, why we have to tip baggers? The reason is because baggers earn their wages from patron tips.

Commissary baggers are self-employed, working under a license agreement with the installation commander. Applicants must present photo identification and a Social Security number to obtain a work license. In most cases, military police will conduct a local records check and work with the Immigration and Naturalization Service as a part of the process. Ordinarily in the United States, bagger applicants must be U.S. citizens or hold a "green card" from the Immigration and Naturalization Service.

Once an installation commander approves a work license, each bagger must sign an agreement with the base commissary. The agreement acknowledges the bagger is not a commissary employee and is not eligible for commissary benefits and incentives, health care or pension. The bagger must also agree to meet store requirements for bagging grocery items and to maintain a neat, clean appearance. Baggers must also declare they will comply with all federal, state and local laws regarding legal employment, income tax and authorized access to the installation.

Baggers perform a very valuable service for commissary customers under a work arrangement that helps keep agency costs and grocery prices low. The commissary website says that customers have the option of bagging their own groceries, but I know I have never been given that option. I plan on asking on my next trip. I use to bag my own groceries in a store in Pennsylvania where I grew up. It saved money on tipping, and I could stuff as many items as I so chose to in my bags. As for baggers at the commissary, how much to tip a bagger is the customer's decision. I have heard some friends tell me that they tip $10.00 each visit, $1.00 a bag, and even $1.00 per cart. So, the amount varies enormously.

A good friend of ours was new to the Navy and took his wife to the commissary to pick up items for a picnic. They went to the check out and shortly after noticed their cart was being pushed by a quiet, little lady. He said to her, "Excuse me, you have my cart." She told him she would take them to his car. He explained there was no need for that, he could take them himself. She proceeded to tell him back that it was her job. Needless to say, this went on for a while. Finally, the young sailor gave in and walked to the car with her. He helped her load the few bags into his car and got in to leave. The bagger knocked on the window and said, "Where's my tip?" He was confused. He told us after this incident that this was his first time to a commissary and he never had heard of such a thing. He said he didn't have any cash on him and had a little, angry woman screaming obscenities to him in her native tongue. It was not a good experience for him, and he hasn't returned to the commissary since. This is a good lesson for all. Don't forget to have cash to pay the baggers. It doesn't have to be much, just a token of appreciation.

Shoppers at military commissaries save an average of more than 30 percent of what they would spend at civilian grocery stores. This is possible because the Defense Commissary Agency follows a policy begun in 1826 of selling goods "at cost" – that is, with no mark-up or profit to the commissary. Commissary shoppers know that a 5-percent surcharge is added at checkout to their grocery bill. (The surcharge is calculated on the total before coupons are deducted.) Not all shoppers know where that money goes, and a lot of shoppers tend to get irritated saying, even though we don't pay tax, we pay a surcharge and it's the same thing. It is most definitely NOT the same thing. It goes right back into the stores, paying for new construction, renovations and repairs, equipment, and store-level information technology systems such as the checkouts. This provides modern facilities for our service members at a reduced cost to taxpayers. Surcharge funds are used for building new stores and modifying existing ones. Commissary customers' surcharge dollars have paid for these projects since 1974. This surcharge is used to make shopping quick, convenient and pleasant, measures that encourage customers to continue using their commissary privilege – which, in turn, helps to generate more surcharge funds! This circle is what keeps the program running so efficiently. Although some surcharges had appeared as early as 1879, the first permanent surcharge was established in 1952, when Congress decided that commissaries should become more self-sustaining. The services were directed to have their commissaries add a 2-percent surcharge to the price of goods to cover costs of purchasing and maintaining equipment and supplies. From the start, the services followed different courses in fulfilling the law. The Army and Air Force chose to use a straight surcharge added to the total bill at checkout. The Navy and Marines Corps used a variable surcharge that was more on some items, less on others, but still averaged the prescribed 2 percent. Then, in 1974, to provide funds for construction and improvements of store facilities, Congress set the surcharge at Army and Air Force stores in the United States at 3 percent (European stores were at one-half percent more). This was increased to 4 percent in 1976 and 5 percent in April 1983. Currently, the surcharge remains at 5 percent at all DeCA stores, stateside and overseas. It has remained the same for over 20 years now. That is a great feat in itself.

Chapter 11

The Aviation Community

After being married for 11 years and receiving his commission in the Navy, my husband had to choose a new platform (or job) for the Navy. He could no longer be aboard submarines as an officer. He didn't have the additional training that a submarine officer has to have. We began to check different fields. Aviation kept coming back to us. There were many options in aviation and they really interested my husband. The more we talked about it, the more it seemed like the adventure to take. I have always been supportive of his choices and try not to sway him either way. Every morning, he's the one who has to go into that job. So it has to be something he likes, or something that interests him no matter what the sacrifice may be for his family. If I asked him, he would never say he would make a choice for that reason and I know he would say it depends what he and I have decided together. But, I always put his dreams and aspirations first. Selflessness is an asset as a Navy wife.

We checked into helicopters and airplanes. Finally, we narrowed it down to P-3s and S-3. The P-3 Orion is a land-based, long-range, anti-submarine warfare (ASW) patrol aircraft. The P-3 provides effective undersea warfare, anti-surface warfare, and command, control, communications, computers, and intelligence, surveillance, and reconnaissance capabilities to naval and joint commanders. S-3 Aircraft are tasked by the Carrier Battle Group Commanders to provide Anti-Submarine Warfare (ASW) and Anti-Surface Warfare (ASUW), surface surveillance and intelligence collection, electronic warfare, mine warfare, coordinated search and rescue, and fleet support missions, including air-wing tanking. They are not land based; they fly on and off aircraft carriers.

From that point, the family came into play. What would be best for our marriage and for our children? After dealing with submarines for 11 years, and the lack of communication we had, we found that the S-3 was not the best for family life from experienced S-3 pilot's and navigator's stories. When it comes to the men, the S-3 is a more exciting ride since they are the pilot's right-hand man. The S-3s were to go on and off carriers; something my husband didn't look forward to would be to still be sleeping on or below water. He wanted to be able to get normal night's sleep. On P-3s he would go to the BOQ (Bachelor Officer Quarters) and it would be like a little studio or 1 bedroom apartment. The S-3s had email, but it could be shut down and there wasn't ability to use a web cam. (In a previous chapter I explained how wonderful having a web cam is for the family. This was one thing we didn't want to give up. It really helps the deployments fly by.) Then the last thing that sold us on P-3 was…per diem. Need I say more? Per diem allowance is a payment in lieu of reimbursement for actual subsistence expenses. It is provided to an employee and eligible dependents for daily expenses while on temporary travel status in the listed localities on official business away from an official post or assignment. Per diem can be mere dollars a day, to hundreds of dollars a day. This is extra income in addition to your regular pay.

We chose P-3s and life was a bit crazy through flight school. We had lived in San Diego, California, for almost 11 years without a move. When my husband accepted the flight program, he had to head to the East Coast for flight school. That wasn't something I was ready to do at the time. I had a great job, our son was in a full immersion school where Spanish was taught as the first language, and my daughter was in a loving daycare. Chip went to flight school in Pensacola, Florida, and we stayed in sunny San Diego. Chip flew out to visit us as much as he could, and my days were busy with the kids. The time flew by fast, but it wasn't fair to our marriage or family life. We were spending so many months separate that we really didn't have much time for anything but work and work alone. It was at that time we decided it was in the best interest in our family if we reunited the two. We packed up the house in San Diego and headed to Pensacola, Florida. It was hard to leave San Diego, but it would have been harder to stay apart any longer.

We moved into a great area in Pensacola, Florida. Perdido was a gorgeous area with white, sandy beaches and not much else. We enjoyed the beach time while we were in Pensacola, Florida. We settled into a routine. Chip would have flights and I would lounge at the pool. We were both doing what we loved. I decided to get a part-time job, and I was really enjoying working part time. Cody was in school, grade 3. This was his first introduction to English in his school day or school curriculum. He excelled and continued to score high grades, even with the new language and the move. McKenna was in part-time preschool on the base. We were just getting settled into our routines when we found out we were transferring to San Antonio, Texas. When I say we had just found out, I mean that literally. We found out we had to be to San Antonio and were to report there in seven days. We had to pack up a 2300 square foot home. We were doing a DITY move again. We ended up losing a lot of money because we had to move before six months of our lease was up and without thirty-days notice.

I was mad because it wasn't our choice; it was the Navy's. But, our realtor (who said he was retired military and said he catered to military families) had not an ounce of compassion when we were faced with this ugly situation. I would give his name to all military families moving to Pensacola to be sure they avoid him. He pretended to be pro-military. It ends up he was only pro-profit. At the time of this ten-day move, there wasn't the protection they now have in effect for military. I wish it were effective then. It would have saved us a few thousand dollars. There is a long, crazy story to the pack up that I won't fully elaborate on at this time. Let's just say, it wasn't a simple "DITY" move. (A DITY move is a move when you do all the moving yourself. Dity stands for Do It Yourself.) The other option is a pack out through the government. In that case, a moving company arrives at your house and packs up every last item you have in your home and loads it into the truck and delivers it to your new home for you. When you hear it, you would say the latter of the two is the way to go. But there are actually many pros and cons to both. Advantages to a DITY move include one word…money. You can make a lot of money when you do a DITY move. Keep in mind; it is a lot of hard work, packing your entire house yourself. But you can always have friends help and you always know that things won't disappear and won't break. If items do break, you know it's nobody's fault but your own. The advantage to a pack out through the government is basically one word also…ease. There is no work on your part except to watch so they don't steal you blind and to be sure your items are packed and labeled correctly. A disadvantage is that they do pack everything. When I say everything except the kitchen sink that is only true unless the kitchen sink isn't bolted down. Otherwise, you may find the kitchen sink as you unpack as well! I have heard of entire bags of trash being found when people unpack—empty pop cans, pizza boxes, and more. So be sure to have everything labeled that goes and everything labeled that stays. A lot of items tend to come up missing when the government packs you out as well. Most common seems to be DVDS, CDS, VIDEOGAMES, and JEWELRY. There is a large list of items that packers cannot pack as well; this includes any items with liquid, including cleaning supplies that unless you can put them in your vehicle will cost a lot to replace. We have done DITY moves for every move in the past fourteen years so far. The only time we didn't was a partial DITY move when Chip had back problems. This was the time when we were halfway through packing and my husband's back went out. We couldn't finish packing the rental truck that we started. We had to call for a partial DITY move and it wasn't going to be as smooth. They came over and had to unpack three-fourths of the boxes that I had already packed. We were so upset at this point, we started giving things away left and right. Whatever fit in, fit in. The rest was going to the trash. We just wanted to get out of there at that point and get to our next destination. The sooner he got to school and finished his training, the sooner we would get to per diem…I mean…the squadron.

Chapter 12

Navy Wife Humor

A Day in the Life of a Navy Wife

I woke up early this morning and I decide to wash my car.

… As I start toward the garage, I notice that there is mail on the hall table.

… I decide to go through the mail before I wash the car.

… I laid my car keys down on the table, put the junk mail in the trash can under the table, and notice that the trash can is full.

… So, I decide to put the bills back on the table and take out the trash first.

… But then I think, since I'm going to be near the mailbox when I take out the trash anyway, I may as well pay the bills first.

… I take my checkbook off the table, and see that there is only one check left.

… My extra checks are in my desk in the study, so I go to my desk where I find the can of Pepsi that I had been drinking.

… I'm going to look for my checks, but first I need to push the Pepsi aside so that I don't accidentally knock it over. I see that the Pepsi is getting warm, and I decide I should put it in the refrigerator to keep it cold.

… As I head toward the kitchen with the Pepsi, a vase of flowers on the counter catches my eye – they need to be watered.

… I set the Pepsi down on the counter, and I discover my reading glasses that I've been searching for all morning.

… I decide I better put them back on my desk, but first I'm going to water the flowers.

… I set the glasses back down on the counter, fill a container with water and suddenly I spot the TV remote someone left on the kitchen table.

… I realize that tonight when we go to watch TV, I will be looking for the remote, but I won't remember that it's on the kitchen table, so I decide to put it back in the den where it belongs, but first I'll water the flowers.

… I splash some water on the flowers, but most of it spills on the floor.

… So, I set the remote back down on the table, get some towels and wipe up the spill.

… Then I head down the hall trying to remember what I was planning to do.

… At the end of the day: the car isn't washed, the bills aren't paid, there is a warm can of Pepsi sitting on the counter, the flowers aren't watered, there is still only one check in my checkbook, I can't find the remote, I can't find my glasses, and I don't remember what I did with the car keys.

… Then when I try to figure out why nothing got done today. I'm really baffled because I know I was busy all day long, and I'm really tired.

… I realize this is a serious problem, and I'll try to get some help for it, but first I'll check my e-mail… maybe my sailor sent me a note!

"The Ten Commandments of a Navy Wife"

1.Thou shalt not write in ink in thy address book. (Why bother? There's an inevitable move in store in three years.)

2.Thou shalt not covet choice duty stations of other uniformed branches of service. You won't get where you want anyway. But you could get where you don't want!

3. Love thy neighbor. (You are stuck with them for at least three years.)

4. Honor thy Commissary and Exchange rules and be courteous on truckload sale days

5.Thou shalt not speed on base, it will effect you and your spouse. (Your spouse more than you.)

6.Thou shall look for the best in every assignment, including the 50%-off rack at the exchange, for all items ending in .96.

7. Thou shall remember all thy friends from all thy stations with greeting cards at Christmas, for thou never knowest when thou may wish to spendeth a night with them while enroute to a new duty station.

8.Be kind and gentle to retired, white-haired Exchange and Commissary customers, because thou too will be a retiree and white haired someday.

9.Thou shalt not curse thy husband when he's on TDY/TAD on a pack out day. (Which inevitably will happen.)

10.Thou must arrive at every new duty station and give it a fair chance... what do you have to lose?

Army/Air Force/ Navy Wives

Three men were sitting together bragging about how they had given their new wives duties.

The first man was in the Army, and bragged that he had told his Army wife she was going to do all the dishes and house cleaning that needed done at their house. He said that it took a couple days but on the third day he came home to a clean house and the dishes were all washed and put away.

The second man was in the Air Force. He bragged that he had given his Air Force wife orders that she was to do all the cleaning, dishes, and the cooking. He told them that the first day he didn't see any results, but the next day it was better. By the third day, his house was clean, the dishes were done, and he had a huge dinner on the table.

The third man, who was in the Navy, boasted that he told his Navy wife that her duties were to keep the house cleaned, dishes washed, lawn mowed, laundry washed and hot meals on the table for every meal. He said the first day he didn't see anything, the second day he didn't see anything, but by the third day most of the swelling had gone down and he could see a little out of his left eye – enough to fix himself a bite to eat, load the dishwasher, and telephone a landscaper.

Chapter 13

Don't Be in a Hurry Going on Base

Don't bother to be in a hurry going on base. It never fails that the times you are running late are the times that things will go haywire. For example, last year my husband was in the hospital for about a week. At the time we had a live-in from Japan for the summer, and I was attempting to show her around. My husband went in the hospital right before a scheduled trip home to visit family in Pennsylvania. It ended up that I had to have my family come down to get my children, so they could spend some time with the grandparents while I tended to Chip in the hospital. He had several failed procedures, and surgeries were beginning. (I won't even write a chapter on some of the medical issues, whereas I could write an entire book on it.) It was a different one every day. I needed to spend my days at the hospital with him. Our visitor from Japan was like family to us. She came in the summer and lived with us. We shared cultures and shared our lives. She lived with us when she was 15, and again when she was 18. She was nervous to go to Pennsylvania without Chip and me, so she opted to stay with us. So, I would spend time with her then rush to see Chip for visiting hours. Then I would run back home to make dinner for our Japanese daughter. On this particular day, I had a lot on my plate. I also knew Chip was getting very sick of hospital food by day four. I told him that after I got everything done here, I would bring him dinner that evening. I rushed out of the house, grabbed dinner for Chip, and rushed to the base. I was cutting it close to the end of visiting hours.

I thought to myself, with my luck the gate will be backed up today. I was just being pessimistic. I got to the base entrance and it was backed up. I kept an eye on the clock. I had a half hour to get dinner to him. I just shook my head at myself thinking how I should have never even thought that. As I sat at the gate barely moving, I started to stress. I really wanted to see Chip and get him a good dinner since he had a surgery in the morning. He wouldn't be able to eat from midnight on, and they said they might have to do another surgery shortly after so he may not have a solid meal for a day or so. I thought to myself, the only thing that could stop me from making it now would be a car inspection. But, in 13 years of marriage, I had never been selected for one up to this point…I had been so lucky. Well, no sooner did I say that than a gate guard motioned my car over to the side. I wasn't mad though. I thought I brought this on myself. All I could do is laugh. And hysterically, mind you. My car was a mess from traveling back and forth to base two to four times a day to see Chip. Oh, boy! My first base car inspection and my car was trashed. They had to literally move bags out of the way and look in them. I had to take everything out of the glove box, which was mostly makeup and tampons that I had in there for my many trips back and forth that week. I had to open the trunk but didn't know where the release button was, so I ended up popping the hood and the gas tank lever too. I was now crying because I was laughing so hard. I looked like a flustered Navy wife who was clueless. Okay, I WAS a flustered Navy wife who was clueless. The one military police asked me what was so funny. *Oh great, now they are going to think I am on something and it will get even worse.* I half expected a breathalyzer at any moment.

But could it? I don't know, but I vowed not to think about it. Threes a charm, but this wouldn't be very charming. I just told the man that I have had one of the worst weeks in my life, and this was just the icing on the cake. He seemed to enjoy my dismay, almost tickled that he chose the right car to frustrate. Everything checked out just fine. They closed my glove box, doors, trunk, hood, and gas tank… and I was on my way to see my husband. Eventually I arrived in his room and tiptoed past the nurse station to bring my husband a cold dinner and a great story about adventures on base. After all, he was a captive audience.

Chapter 14

Do You Know the Flag Rules and Regulations?

There are a lot of rules that go along with the use of the American flag. It's amazing how many there are that are being misused. Read along and see how many you are familiar with, and how many are new to you. I see the American flag abused every day. Do you?

When the flag is displayed over the middle of the street, it should be suspended vertically with the union to the north in an east and west street or to the east in a north and south street.

When the United States Flag is displayed with another flag against a wall from crossed staffs, should be on the right, the flag's own, and its staff should be in front of the staff of the other flag. No exceptions.

When flown at half-staff, the dear America flag should be first hoisted to the peak for an instant and then lowered to the half-staff position. The flag should be again raised to the peak before it is lowered for the day. By "half-staff" is meant lowering the flag to one-half the distance between the top and bottom of the staff. Crepe streamers may be affixed to spear heads or flagstaffs in a parade only by order of the President of the United States.

When flags of States, cities, or localities, or pennants of societies are flown with the flag of the United States, the latter should always be at the peak. When the flags are flown from adjacent staffs, the flag of the United States should always be hoisted first and lowered last. No such flag or pennant may be placed above the flag of the United States or to the right of the flag of the United States. No exceptions.

When the flag is suspended over a sidewalk from a rope extending from a house to a pole at the edge of the sidewalk, the flag should be hoisted out from the building, union first.

When the U.S. flag is displayed from a staff projecting horizontally or at an angle from the windowsill, balcony, or front of a building, the union of the flag should be placed at the peak of the staff *unless* the flag is at half-staff.

When using a flag to cover a casket, it should be so placed that the union is at the head and over the left shoulder. The flag should not be lowered into the grave or ever allowed to touch the ground. No exceptions.

When the flag is displayed in a manner other than by being flown from a staff, it should be displayed flat, whether indoors or out. When displayed either horizontally or vertically against a wall, the union should be uppermost and to the flag's own right, to the observer's left. When displayed in a window, it should be displayed in the same way, which is with the union or blue field to the left of the observer in the street. When draping is desired, bunting of blue, white and red should be used, but never the flag.

When an American flag is carried in a procession with another flag, or flags, it should be either on the marching right; the flag's own right, or, if there is a line of other flags, in front of the center of that line.

The flag of the United States of America should always be at the center and at the highest point of the group when a number of flags of States or localities or pennants of societies are grouped and displayed

When flags of two or more nations are displayed, they are to be flown from separate staffs of the same height. The flags should be of equal size. International usage forbids the display of the flag of one nation above that of another nation in time of peace.

When displayed from a staff in a church or public auditorium on or off a podium, the flag of the United States of America should always hold the position of superior prominence and in the position of honor at the clergyman's or speaker's right as he faces the audience. Any other flag so displayed should be placed on the left of the clergyman or speaker or to the right of the audience.

When the flag is displayed on a car, the staff shall be fixed firmly to the chassis or clamped to the right fender.

When a flag is hung in a window, place the blue union in the upper left, as viewed from the street.

The proper procedure to retire an American flag when it is in such condition that it is no longer a fitting emblem for display is that it should be destroyed in a dignified way, preferably by burning. We recommend that you contact your local VFW Chapter and ask them for help properly disposing of your flag. And be sure to consider providing a small donation to them for their assistance. Or you can contact your local Elks Lodge (who created the idea of Flag Day, established officially by President Truman, himself a member of the Elks) or the American Legion. Some Boy Scout and Girl Scout troops also can provide this service.

Q. Is it appropriate to fly a flag that has fewer than 50 stars? Yes. There is nothing wrong in flying an historic flag.

Q. Do I need to destroy a flag if it touches the ground? No. You should, of course, try to avoid having the flag touch the ground. But if it does, you should correct the situation immediately. If the flag has been dirtied, you should clean it by hand with a mild soap solution and dry it well before returning it to use.

Q. Why do some flags have gold trim or fringe on them? What does it mean? The gold trim is found on ceremonial flags, to be used indoors and for ceremonies only. They originally were used on military flags. The fringe has no specific significance, but is considered to be within the guidelines of proper flag etiquette. There is nothing in the flag code indicating that the fringe is for federal government flags only. The Internet contains many sites that claim that the fringe indicates martial law or that the Constitution does not apply in that area. These are entirely unfounded and should be dismissed as urban legends.

Q. Should I fly my flag at half-mast on September 11 and at what time? Yes, by proclamation, "I call upon all Americans to display the flag at half-staff from their homes on that day and to observe a moment of silence beginning at 8:46 a.m. eastern daylight time to honor the innocent victims who lost their lives as a result of the terrorist attacks of September 11, 2001." You can read the entire proclamation on the Internet.

Q. Upon the death of a sitting or former President, how long does the flag fly at half-mast? For a Vice-President? The flag should fly at half-mast for 30 days for the death of a sitting or former President. Ten days for the death of a Vice President.

Q. Can my company decide to fly our flag at half-mast for a former employee? No. Only the President of the US or your state governor can order the flag lowered to half-staff.

Q. I am thinking of getting a flag tattoo. Is it okay? There is nothing in the Flag Code about tattoos forbidding it. It only raises a question of respect for the flag. In this case one person's respect is another's disrespect.

Q. What is the meaning of the folds in a flag-folding ceremony? There is no reference to meaning of the folds in the Flag Code. Although, did you know that a properly proportioned flag will fold 13 times on the triangles, representing the 13 original colonies. When finally complete the triangular folded flag is emblematical of the tri-corner hat worn by the Patriots of the American Revolution. When folded, no red or white stripe is to be evident leaving only the honor field of blue and stars. You can check on the Internet for the entire procedure of the flag-folding ceremony. The story behind each fold is heart wrenching.

Q. Does the ball ornament atop a flagpole contain a razor, lighter, and flare? No. This is just an urban legend. One explanation is that the myth started during the Cold War and that the objects were to be used to destroy the flag in the event of a Soviet invasion. Of course, the ball ornament predates the Cold War by many years

Q. Is it okay to have a flag t-shirt with words written on it? No, the flag should never be worn and no, the flag should never have marks or words written upon it "The flag should never be used as wearing apparel." Section 8g: "The flag should never have placed upon it, nor on any part of it, nor attached to it any mark, insignia, letter, word, figure, design, picture, or drawing of any nature."

Q. Is it okay to use flag napkins or flag paper plates? It is written that it should not be printed or otherwise impressed on paper napkins or boxes or anything that is designed for temporary use and discard. But, it is done every day and on the 4th of July opt for red or white or blue plates instead of the preprinted flag ones.

Q. Is it okay for an advertisement to use the flag? No again. The flag should never be used for advertising purposes in any manner.

Q. Where does the flag fly 24 hours a day? It is written that when a patriotic effect is desired, the flag may be displayed for twenty-four hours a day if properly illuminated during the hours of darkness. Of course, it always flies 24 hours a day on the moon. There is an elite group where, by executive order, the flag is to fly 24 hours a day. Some of those places are listed later in the chapter

Q. What does "properly illuminated" mean? Section 6a: "When a patriotic effect is desired, the flag may be displayed twenty-four hours a day if properly illuminated during the hours of darkness." The Flag Rules offer no additional guidance on this question. We interpret this to mean that there is either a light directly upon the flag or that there is sufficient local lighting to make the flag easily visible at night.

Q. When children paint the American flag is that against the Flag rules and regulations? Respectfully featuring the American flag in artwork is a wonderful thing and should be encouraged. We would hope that the artwork is preserved and displayed proudly by the young artists and their families.

Q. What does the Flag Code say about displaying the flag horizontally, as before a football game? Section 8c. reads, "The flag should never be carried flat or horizontally, but always aloft and free."

Q. Why is the flag sometimes backwards on the side of airplanes, buses, and other vehicles? The flag decals have the union (the blue area with the stars) on the side closer to the front of the plane. On the plane's left, the decal shows the flag with the union at the left, as usual. On the plane's right side, the union is on the right. This is done so that the flag looks as if it is blowing in the wind created by the forward movement. You can see this on cars and trucks as well.

Q. What is the proper way to wear a flag patch on one's shoulder sleeve? To wear our country's flag properly, the field of stars should be worn closest to your heart. Thus, if your patch is to be worn on your LEFT sleeve, use a left flag. For patches worn on your RIGHT sleeve, use a "right" or "reversed field" flag. Since the law does not specifically address the positioning of the patch, a decision is left to the discretion of the organization prescribing the wear. Some elect to use the "left" flag on both sleeves. [Note: Many states and cities have ordinances pertaining to the use of the flag; you may wish to contact the Attorney General of your state or the City Attorney's office regarding this matter.] If you are planning to wear only one patch, it is recommended that you wear a "left" flag on your left sleeve. Military guidelines specify that in support of joint- or multi-national operations, the "right" flag is worn on the right sleeve, 1/4" below the shoulder seam or 1/8" below any required unit patches.

Q. Isn't the American flag stamp in violation of the flag rules? This question has been asked by dozens. The answer appears to be yes. Section 8e reads, "The flag should never be ... used ... in such a manner as to permit it to be easily torn, soiled, or damaged in any way." Section 8g. reads, "The flag should never have placed upon it, nor on any part of it, nor attached to it any mark ... of any nature." 8i. reads, "[The flag] should not be printed or otherwise impressed on ... anything that is designed for temporary use and discard."

Flag Rules and Regulations

By Executive Order, the flag flies 24 hours a day at the following locations:

The Betsy Ross House, Philadelphia, Pennsylvania

The White House, Washington, D.C.

U.S. Capitol, Washington, D.C.

Washington Monument, Washington, D.C.

Iwo Jima Memorial to U.S. Marines, Arlington, Virginia

Battleground in Lexington, MA (site of first shots in the Revolutionary War)

Winter encampment cabins, Valley Forge, Pennsylvania

Fort McHenry, Baltimore, Maryland (a flag flying over Fort McHenry after a battle during the War of 1812 provided the inspiration for "The Star Spangled Banner."

The Star-Spangled Banner Flag House, Baltimore, Maryland (site where the famed flag over Fort McHenry was sewn)

Jenny Wade House in Gettysburg, Pennsylvania (Jenny Wade was the only civilian killed at the battle of Gettysburg)

U.S.S. Arizona Memorial, Pearl Harbor, Hawaii

All custom points and points of entry into the United States

Title 4, Chapter 1: The Flag

Sec. 1. — Flag; stripes and stars on

The flag of the United States shall be thirteen horizontal stripes, alternate red and white; and the union of the flag shall be forty-eight stars *[**Note** that sec. 2 which follows provides for additional stars. Today the flag has fifty stars representing the fifty states – Webmaster]*, white in a blue field

Sec. 2. — Same; additional stars

On the admission of a new State into the Union one star shall be added to the union of the flag; and such addition shall take effect on the fourth day of July then next succeeding such admission

*Sec. 3. *[This section relates only to the District of Columbia and is being omitted for this publication]*

Sec. 4. — Pledge of allegiance to the flag; manner of delivery

The Pledge of Allegiance to the Flag, "I pledge allegiance to the Flag of the United States of America, and to the Republic for which it stands, one Nation under God, indivisible, with liberty and justice for all.", should be rendered by standing at attention facing the flag with the right hand over the heart. When not in uniform, men should remove their headdress with their right hand and hold it at the left shoulder, the hand being over the heart. Persons in uniform should remain silent, face the flag, and render the military salute

Sec. 5. — Display and use of flag by civilians; codification of rules and customs; definition

The following codification of existing rules and customs pertaining to the display and use of the flag of the United States of America be, and it is hereby, established for the use of such civilians or civilian groups or organizations as may not be required to conform with regulations promulgated by one or more executive departments of the Government of the United States. The flag of the United States for the purpose of this chapter shall be defined according to title 4, United States Code, Chapter 1, Section 1 and Section 2 and Executive Order 10834 issued pursuant thereto.

Sec. 6. — Time and occasions for display

It is the universal custom to display the flag only from sunrise to sunset on buildings and on stationary flagstaffs in the open. However, when a patriotic effect is desired, the flag may be displayed twenty-four hours a day if properly illuminated during the hours of darkness.

The flag should be hoisted briskly and lowered ceremoniously.

The flag should not be displayed on days when the weather is inclement, except when an all-weather flag is displayed.

The flag should be displayed on all days, especially on:
New Year's Day, January 1
Inauguration Day, January 20
Martin Luther King Jr.'s birthday, third Monday in January
Lincoln's Birthday, February 12
Washington's Birthday, third Monday in February
Easter Sunday (variable)
Mother's Day, second Sunday in May
Armed Forces Day, third Saturday in May
Memorial Day (half-staff until noon), the last Monday in May
Flag Day, June 14
Independence Day, July 4
Labor Day, first Monday in September
Constitution Day, September 17
Columbus Day, second Monday in October
Navy Day, October 27
Veterans Day, November 11
Thanksgiving Day, fourth Thursday in November
Christmas Day, December 25
and such other days as may be proclaimed by the President of the United States
the birthdays of States (date of admission) and on State holidays.

The flag should be displayed daily on or near the main administration building of every public institution.

The flag should be displayed in or near every polling place on election days.

The flag should be displayed during school days in or near every schoolhouse.

Sec. 7. — Position and manner of display

The flag should not be displayed on a float in a parade except from a staff, or as provided in subsection (i) of this section.

The flag should not be draped over the hood, top, sides, or back of a vehicle or of a railroad train or a boat. When the flag is displayed on a motorcar, the staff shall be fixed firmly to the chassis or clamped to the right fender.

No other flag or pennant should be placed above or, if on the same level, to the right of the flag of the United States of America, except during church services conducted by naval chaplains at sea, when the church pennant may be flown above the flag during church services for the personnel of the Navy. No person shall display the flag of the United Nations or any other national or international flag equal, above, or in a position of superior prominence or honor to, or in place of, the flag of the United States at any place within the United States or any Territory or possession thereof: Provided, That nothing in this section shall make unlawful the continuance of the practice heretofore followed of displaying the flag of the United Nations in a position of superior prominence or honor, and other national flags in positions of equal prominence or honor, with that of the flag of the United States at the headquarters of the United Nations.

The flag of the United States of America, when it is displayed with another flag against a wall from crossed staffs, should be on the right, the flag's own right, and its staff should be in front of the staff of the other flag.

The flag of the United States of America should be at the center and at the highest point of the group when a number of flags of States or localities or pennants of societies are grouped and displayed from staffs.

When flags of States, cities, or localities, or pennants of societies are flown on the same halyard with the flag of the United States, the latter should always be at the peak. When the flags are flown from adjacent staffs, the flag of the United States should be hoisted first and lowered last. No such flag or pennant may be placed above the flag of the United States or to the United States flag's right.

When flags of two or more nations are displayed, they are to be flown from separate staffs of the same height. The flags should be of approximately equal size. International usage forbids the display of the flag of one nation above that of another nation in time of peace.

When the flag of the United States is displayed from a staff projecting horizontally or at an angle from the window sill, balcony, or front of a building, the union of the flag should be placed at the peak of the staff unless the flag is at half-staff. When the flag is suspended over a sidewalk from a rope extending from a house to a pole at the edge of the sidewalk, the flag should be hoisted out, union first, from the building.

When displayed either horizontally or vertically against a wall, the union should be uppermost and to the flag's own right, that is, to the observer's left. When displayed in a window, the flag should be displayed in the same way, with the union or blue field to the left of the observer in the street.

When the flag is displayed over the middle of the street, it should be suspended vertically with the union to the north in an east and west street or to the east in a north and south street.

When used on a speaker's platform, the flag, if displayed flat, should be displayed above and behind the speaker. When displayed from a staff in a church or public auditorium, the flag of the United States of America should hold the position of superior prominence, in advance of the audience, and in the position of honor at the clergyman's or speaker's right as he faces the audience. Any other flag so displayed should be placed on the left of the clergyman or speaker or to the right of the audience.

The flag should form a distinctive feature of the ceremony of unveiling a statue or monument, but it should never be used as the covering for the statue or monument.

The flag, when flown at half-staff, should be first hoisted to the peak for an instant and then lowered to the half-staff position. The flag should be again raised to the peak before it is lowered for the day. On Memorial Day the flag should be displayed at half-staff until noon only, then raised to the top of the staff. By order of the President, the flag shall be flown at half-staff upon the death of principal figures of the United States Government and the Governor of a State, territory, or possession, as a mark of respect to their memory. In the event of the death of other officials or foreign dignitaries, the flag is to be displayed at half-staff according to Presidential instructions or orders, or in accordance with recognized customs or practices not inconsistent with law. In the event of the death of a present or former official of the government of any State, territory, or possession of the United States, the Governor of that State, territory, or possession may proclaim that the National flag shall be flown at half-staff. The flag shall be flown at half-staff 30 days from the death of the President or a former President; 10 days from the day of death of the Vice President, the Chief Justice or a retired Chief Justice of the United States, or the Speaker of the House of Representatives; from the day of death until interment of an Associate Justice of the Supreme Court, a Secretary of an executive or military department, a former Vice President, or the Governor of a State, territory, or possession; and on the day of death and the following day for a Member of Congress. The flag shall be flown at half-staff on Peace Officers Memorial Day, unless that day is also Armed Forces Day. As used in this subsection – the term "half-staff" means the position of the flag when it is one-half the distance between the top and bottom of the staff; the term "executive or military department" means any agency listed under sections 101 and 102 of title 5, United States Code; and the term "Member of Congress" means a Senator, a Representative, a Delegate, or the Resident Commissioner from Puerto Rico.

When the flag is used to cover a casket, it should be so placed that the union is at the head and over the left shoulder. The flag should not be lowered into the grave or allowed to touch the ground.

When the flag is suspended across a corridor or lobby in a building with only one main entrance, it should be suspended vertically with the union of the flag to the observer's left upon entering. If the building has more than one main entrance, the flag should be suspended vertically near the center of the corridor or lobby with the union to the north, when entrances are to the east and west or to the east when entrances are to the north and south. If there are entrances in more than two directions, the union should be to the east

Sec. 8. — Respect for flag

No disrespect should be shown to the flag of the United States of America; the flag should not be dipped to any person or thing. Regimental colors, State flags, and organization or institutional flags are to be dipped as a mark of honor.

The flag should never be displayed with the union down, except as a signal of dire distress in instances of extreme danger to life or property.

The flag should never touch anything beneath it, such as the ground, the floor, water, or merchandise.

The flag should never be carried flat or horizontally, but always aloft and free.

The flag should never be used as wearing apparel, bedding, or drapery. It should never be festooned, drawn back, nor up, in folds, but always allowed to fall free. Bunting of blue, white, and red, always arranged with the blue above, the white in the middle, and the red below, should be used for covering a speaker's desk, draping the front of the platform, and for decoration in general.

The flag should never be fastened, displayed, used, or stored in such a manner as to permit it to be easily torn, soiled, or damaged in any way.

The flag should never be used as a covering for a ceiling.

The flag should never have placed upon it, nor on any part of it, nor attached to it any mark, insignia, letter, word, figure, design, picture, or drawing of any nature.

The flag should never be used as a receptacle for receiving, holding, carrying, or delivering anything.

The flag should never be used for advertising purposes in any manner whatsoever. It should not be embroidered on such articles as cushions or handkerchiefs and the like, printed or otherwise impressed on paper napkins or boxes or anything that is designed for temporary use and discard. Advertising signs should not be fastened to a staff or halyard from which the flag is flown.

No part of the flag should ever be used as a costume or athletic uniform. However, a flag patch may be affixed to the uniform of military personnel, firemen, policemen, and members of patriotic organizations. The flag represents a living country and is itself considered a living thing. Therefore, the lapel flag pin being a replica, should be worn on the left lapel near the heart.

The flag, when it is in such condition that it is no longer a fitting emblem for display, should be destroyed in a dignified way, preferably by burning

Sec. 9. — Conduct during hoisting, lowering or passing of flag

During the ceremony of hoisting or lowering the flag or when the flag is passing in a parade or in review, all persons present except those in uniform should face the flag and stand at attention with the right hand over the heart. Those present in uniform should render the military salute. When not in uniform, men should remove their headdress with their right hand and hold it at the left shoulder, the hand being over the heart. Aliens should stand at attention. The salute to the flag in a moving column should be rendered at the moment the flag passes

Sec. 10. — Modification of rules and customs by President

Any rule or custom pertaining to the display of the flag of the United States of America, set forth herein, may be altered, modified, or repealed, or additional rules with respect thereto may be prescribed, by the Commander in Chief of the Armed Forces of the United States, whenever he deems it to be appropriate or desirable; and any such alteration or additional rule shall be set forth in a proclamation.

References

US CODE COLLECTION, Cornell University
US Code, GPO
Army Regulation 840-10 [PDF Acrobat format.
This material is copyright by, and used with permission of, the Independence Hall Association.
For further information, visit the Independence Hall Association's Home Page on the World Wide Web at http://www.ushistory.org.

Chapter 15

Then and Now

**The Navy Then and Now,
Oh, How Times Have Changed**

Then – if a sailor smoked, he/she had an ashtray on his/her desk.
Now – if a sailor smokes he/she is sent outside and far away from civilization

Then – Mail took weeks to arrive aboard the ship.
Now – Every time the ship nears land, everyone is topside seeing if his or her cell phone works.

Then – If a sailor left the ship it was in Blues or Whites.
Now – The only time they wear Blues or Whites is for ceremonies.

Then – Sailors wore bellbottoms everywhere on the ship.
Now – Bellbottoms are gone from the Navy, but 14 year-old girls wear them everywhere.

Then – Sailors wore a "dixie cup" all day, with every uniform.
Now – It's not required, and they have a choice of various head wear.

Then – If you said "damn," people knew you were annoyed and avoided you.
Now – If you say "dam" you'd better be talking about a hydroelectric plant.

Then -The Ship's Yeoman had a typewriter on his desk for doing daily reports.
Now – Everyone has a computer with Internet access. (And they wonder why no work gets done.)

Then – We painted pictures of pretty girls on airplanes to remind us of home.
Now – We put the real thing in the drivers seat!

Then – Your girlfriend was at home, praying you would return alive.
Now – She is on the same ship working alongside you.

Then – Canteens were made out of steel and you could heat coffee or hot chocolate in them.
Now – Canteens are made of plastic. You can't heat them because they'll melt, and anything inside always tastes like plastic.

Then – Enemy intelligence was collected and analyzed.
Now – The crew's urine is collected and analyzed.

Then – If a sailor didn't act correctly and obey the rules, he'd be put on extra duty until he squared away.
Now – If he doesn't behave, a paper trail is started that follows him forever.

Then – Medals were awarded to heroes who saved lives at the risk of their own.

Now – Medals are awarded to people who show up for work most of the time.

Then – The crew slept in a barracks, like a soldier.

Now – They sleep in a co-ed dormitory, like a college kid.

Then – Sailors ate in a Mess Hall. The food was free and they could generally eat their fill.

Now – They dine in a Dining Facility. There are different foods with different costs.

Then – If a sailor wanted to relax, he went to the Rec Center, played some pool, smoked, drank beer, and told sea stories.

Now -They can go to a local Community Center (if they can find one) and pay to play pool. Not much comes for free anymore.

Then – If a sailor wanted a couple beers and some social conversation he could go to the EM club while officers to the "O" club where a glass of beer was a quarter.

Now – The beer will cost two bucks and someone will be watching your drinking pattern.

Chip and Jasa

Jasa, Chip, McKenna, and Cody

Chip, Jasa, Cody and McKenna

Printed in the United States
153842LV00002B/64/A